Faeries & Elementals
For Beginners

Photo © Sarah O' Brien

About the Author

Alexandra Chauran is a second-generation fortuneteller, a third degree elder High Priestess of British Traditional Wicca, and the Queen of a coven. As a professional psychic intuitive for over a decade, she serves thousands of clients in the Seattle area and globally through her website. She is certified in tarot and has been interviewed on National Public Radio and other major media outlets. Alexandra is currently pursuing a doctoral degree, lives in Issaquah, Washington, and can be found online at EarthShod.com.

Faeries & Elementals

For Beginners

Learn About & Communicate
With Nature Spirits

ALEXANDRA CHAURAN

Llewellyn Publications
Woodbury, Minnesota

FIRST EDITION
Sixth Printing, 2020

Book format by Bob Gaul
Cover art: Foggy country road © iStockphoto.com/Ben Klaus
Cover design by Ellen Lawson
Editing by Laura Graves

Llewellyn Publications is a registered trademark of Llewellyn Worldwide Ltd.

Library of Congress Cataloging-in-Publication Data
The Library of Congress has already cataloged an earlier printing under LCCN: 2013022276

Llewellyn Worldwide Ltd. does not participate in, endorse, or have any authority or responsibility concerning private business transactions between our authors and the public.

All mail addressed to the author is forwarded, but the publisher cannot, unless specifically instructed by the author, give out an address or phone number.

Any Internet references contained in this work are current at publication time, but the publisher cannot guarantee that a specific location will continue to be maintained. Please refer to the publisher's website for links to authors' websites and other sources.

Llewellyn Publications
A Division of Llewellyn Worldwide Ltd.
2143 Wooddale Drive
Woodbury, MN 55125-2989
www.llewellyn.com

Printed in the United States of America

Other books by Alexandra Chauran

Crystal Ball Reading for Beginners
Have You Been Hexed?
Palmistry Every Day
So You Want to Be a Psychic Intuitive?

contents

introduction

Are there winged and glowing beings floating through the air, just on the edge of your field of vision and your imagination? What strange and wonderful creatures may exist in the deepest depths of the ocean, beyond where humans have the capacity to discover? Is there intelligence in the earth or life in a crackling fire? Discovering elementals and faeries for the first time is like exploring the boundaries of where reality, imagination, and spiritual truth meet and intersect. By the time you finish this book, you'll be ready to start exploring what you believe.

What Are Faeries?
In popular culture, faeries take on the familiar form of small, winged creatures. Indeed, many cultures have versions of faeries

that fit the familiar profile. However, "faerie" (or "fairy") is an umbrella term that covers many mythological creatures that can range from beautiful sea beasts to nightmarish monsters that stomp through the night.

Faeries are the way that people have understood some of the more magical and mysterious forces of life and nature, from the birth of a particularly beautiful child as a faerie blessing, to a terrible crop yield as a faerie curse. Faeries are the faces we put on real phenomenon so we can propitiate them, ward them away, or even bargain with them.

What Are Elementals?

Elementals are beings made up of energy. Of course, they are not composed of the energy we speak about in scientific terms, like electricity, but spiritual energy. Spiritual energy, or *chi*, is the life force within all things, and the potential used in magic to manifest one's desires. In the case of elementals, their energy can be used to manifest their desires and your own. The trick is to make sure that you and the elementals share the same goals.

If you were to gather all the faerie creatures that have ever been imagined across time and cultures, they would all fit into one or more of only four categories: earth, air, fire, and water. For the purposes of predicting the behavior and needs of elementals, they have been classified by their element. Although this would imply that there are only four species of elementals, some cultures label any spiritual entity that watches over any of those domains as an elemental. For example, a deva might be considered an elemental since it loves the earth. In the context of this book, I will instead choose to lump most natural spiritual entities into the "faeries" category so that you can read about them earlier in the book. The term "elementals" will focus on gnomes, sylphs, salamanders, and undines.

Significance of the Elements and How Elementals Came to Be

Long before the chemical elements were organized into a periodic table, people were trying to classify things on earth. For alchemists—primitive chemists and philosopher magicians that they were—the four elements of earth, air, fire, and water were assumed to be the building blocks for all of creation. Aristotle became one of the first to describe the behavior of elementals, in that they belonged to their respective dominions and naturally were attracted back to their sphere of influence if left alone. Therefore, it takes effort and sometimes even force to make an elemental do something it is not already doing by virtue of its own state of being.

With a little thought, everything could be fit into elemental components. For example, a human is made up of all of four alchemical elements. We breathe air in and out of our bodies. Our blood, saliva, and other fluids are attributed to water. The solid body itself is made up of the element of earth, and the heat that comes from our metabolism is from an inner source of the element of fire.

Though the periodic table of the elements does not include any of these four elements, since they are outdated for the uses of modern science, ceremonial magicians have continued an unbroken tradition of using the four elements in magic as well as for important ritual structures that are fundamental to understanding of Western magic's concepts. Many Western forms of witchcraft borrowed heavily from established ceremonial magic traditions, and these included the use of elements.

Not only did ceremonial magicians develop a ritual structure that used the four elements as building blocks in the architecture of magical structures called circles, but they also used a mode of communication with magical entities that was quite forceful and authoritative, calling on elementals to do their bidding and establishing one of the first ways that people could work directly with elementals by taking them out of their element, so to speak.

Elementals in a Religious Context

While ceremonial magicians and many other historical practitioners of magic did not use elementals in the context of worship, elementals have found their place in many world religions and in modern witchcraft's spiritual component. As soon as elementals became more than just a magical hypothesis, they began to become inextricably bound to nature. Ceremonialist use of elementals remains largely relegated to symbolism within ritual constructs. Yet people from various faith traditions, including Buddhism and Neopaganism, in addition to practitioners of traditional medicines, commune with elementals outdoors among the woods, streams, oceans, lakes, and the furious weather of the natural world.

What Should Your Focus Be? How Can You Incorporate Them into Your Life?

Although elementals find their way into practical use in many religious and healing arts, they are largely theoretical in nature. Understanding elementals is to philosophize about all of existence and how it fits into various categories of understanding. If you are a deep thinker, and enjoy philosophy and theology, the four traditional elementals may be the right focus for you. By using elementals, you can analyze your life critically using the elementals as a tool to rebalance and to seek blessings.

If, however, you find that elementals feel too impersonal, and you don't want to devote your entire life to their study, you would do best to focus on faeries. These beings are the fun and intriguing faces of elementals that can bring them more easily into everyday life. By incorporating faeries into your daily routine, you can add a little magic and perhaps get a little closer to nature in the process. Faeries let you dip your toe into understanding elementals, and can help the beginner to get started figuring out what you truly believe.

Why Work with Elementals and Other Mythological Creatures?

Why should anyone choose to invoke mysterious and possibly dangerous magical wildlife? It may seem tantamount to inviting a rabid squirrel into your home. Whether the idea sounds fun or daunting, it is impossible to ignore the power that the four elements have as a concept. The four elements persist because they work to solve life's problems, and if they work they should continue to be used.

With the use of elementals, you have additional energetic and enthusiastic little friends that can help you. Not only do many hands make light work, but the focus and drive to do what is in their true nature to do can make elementals obsessively devoted to your goals when appropriate aims are selected for appropriate elementals.

As in ancient times, the modern world is still full of mystery. Faeries and elementals are some models that can still be used to explain the way things work. Entertaining the idea of mythological creatures can bring light and magic to everyday situations, such as losing track of your car keys and blaming it on the pixies. And, in some instances, the mythological explanation makes a lot more sense than any rational one…especially if you specifically remember setting your keys down in a specific place only to find them transported to a surprisingly high shelf.

Are They "Real"?

The real question that plagues the more literal-minded type of person reading this book is whether or not little people or elementals are real. Of course, this depends on what you mean by the term "real." Naturally, faeries and gnomes are not the same ones that you see animated on television or depicted by lawn ornaments. Beyond that extreme, though, the lines intersect between inspiration, imagination, fable, and metaphor. Faeries and elementals have established themselves as workable archetypes for understanding the incomprehensible, and have rightfully earned a place in the real-world practices of rational adults.

Speaking of archetypes, I should explain how they are different from thoughtforms. Often, archetypes feel a little more "real" in the practical context of working with them. A thoughtform is an idea that can take the form of an entity, like an elemental, but thoughtforms are fueled by the energy of the person thinking about the idea. Usually, the thoughtform exists for a short time so a specific task may be performed. Once the goal is completed and the mind stops feeding energy into the thoughtform, it dissipates. Elementals can also carry out goals, and they are also representative of many ideas. In this way, elementals already exist as archetypes in the human collective unconscious, and can be called upon as needed without ceasing to exist when an individual's goal has been achieved.

What You Will Learn, Know, and Be Able to Do

Through this book, I will attempt to educate the reader a bit on the history and mythology of elementals and faeries without getting too bogged down in what other people believe. More importantly, I will help you to personify the concepts behind magical creatures so that they can become practical and useful tools and companions to your magical work.

By the end of this book, you will understand which duties fit what elementals and faeries best, how to communicate with them, and how to get them to help you with problems in everyday life. You'll get a handle on where elementals and faeries fit into your own psychology. You'll learn how they can impact your spiritual practice by giving it a structure, philosophy, and multiple ways of going about getting what you want in a world that can be chaotic and have a mind of its own, just like the entities you will come to know.

Most of all, I'd like you to meet elementals and faeries in the common ground of your own mind, your environment, or wherever your biggest hopes and fears collide. I want you to see helpful entities, with your mind's eye or otherwise, and to startle yourself with observations of an exotic wildlife of mythological proportions. Working with elementals and faeries is something you have to see to believe. Jump right in and get started with some steps you can take to work directly with magical entities. The results you'll find in your own life will speak for themselves.

one

Getting Started
with Faeries

Jane loved playing with her kids and how the real world and imagination were always intertwined. As an artist and writer, Jane wanted to keep inspirational traditions woven into her family's culture at all times. Instead of waiting for Santa to come to town to put out milk and cookies, Sarah's two daughters helped put out a family offering to the faeries in the garden every night before bedtime.

At dinner, a small plate for the faeries rested always in the middle of the table. Before digging in to eat, each family member placed a crumb of each food they were going to eat. Jane's youngest, Madison, added an extra big glass of milk to ask the faeries to bring back her favorite doll that had gone missing. After dinner, *her eldest, Tammy, took the plate to the center of the garden in the front yard and left it on a rock right under the bird bath.*

Jane smiled as she watched her children giggling and dancing wildly around the bird bath, thanking the faeries for flowers and kittens and everything they thought was joyous and good. A flicker of light caught Jane's eye. Was it a reflection of light off the water? A glowing dust mote seemed to dance in the orange glow of the setting sun as if it had a mind of its own. Jane sensed a feeling of well-being and happiness. "Tammy, Maddie!" she said. "Did you see a faerie in the sunlight too?" Tammy stopped dancing and hugged her little sister, cocking her head at her mother quizzically. "Of course, Mommy, they're always there."

Not all spiritual entities found in nature can be simply classified as a single elemental of one of the four elements. The catchall term of "faeries" includes many other creatures, although they may be more detailed expressions of the classical elements. In this chapter, we'll examine the outliers called faeries as a whole, and then I will give some example of especially common faeries in folklore, as well as a few that are particularly elemental in nature. Some faeries fit the stereotype seen in popular culture of small winged people. Others may look not humanoid at all in their associated myths and legends. Many faeries are adorable and friendly folk, while many others may be mischievous or downright dangerous and mean.

In general, well-meaning faeries are lumped into the Seelie category, while those that probably wish you harm are called Unseelie. Think of them as a huge kingdom of creatures. Just as you can't characterize all animals as "nice," living things that would make fine pets, faeries vary widely depending on the culture and region that gave them life in literature and through spirituality. Nearly all faeries have been given a bad reputation at some point or another, simply because they are given to pleasures like music and dancing, feasting and drinking, playing and partying. At various points in history, all of those joys have been forbidden or enjoyed only in moderation by people who often thought that faeries demonstrated a disgraceful lack of restraint.

Yet as unspecific as the concept of faeries may be, some magical practitioners connect with them on a deep level. If each of the four elemental types gives a person greater understanding and control of the building blocks of the universe, you can think of faeries as a tangible conceptual connection with nature and the energetic force of life itself. Even if you don't believe in faeries in the literal sense, it can help to personify the very real powers they represent.

How You Can Communicate with Faeries and Incorporate Them into Your Life

Adding faerie energies to your life can be very useful, and not just because faeries are pretty and cute. Befriending faeries, or at least getting on their good side, can spare you from their faerie misdeeds and gain you some magical help. Faeries might help with chores around the house and garden, and even assist in finding lost objects. Some might say that those lost objects were the very things stolen by the faeries in the first place, so I'll leave it to you to decide whether they are doing you a favor by returning them. Faeries are healing creatures, especially for those suffering emotional or spiritual afflictions, as they can bring joy back into life.

Faeries are feral creatures, so they are intimately in tune with both wild and domesticated animals. As such, faeries are naturally inclined to help animals and can be asked to help as intermediaries when you are having a problem with an animal in your care. For example, if your dog seems depressed, ask the faeries to help you find out what's wrong and let them be your dog's interpreter in your dreams. Requesting their help to heal a sick horse can help the veterinarian's work bring about results more quickly. You can ask for the aid of the faeries when dealing with wild animals as well, asking them to keep dangerous or annoying animals away from your home.

As much as faeries are ministers to animals, they are even more in tune with plants, allowing gardens, orchards and crops to grow and thrive with abundance. Consider inviting faeries into your life by designing a garden just for them. A faerie garden should be mostly flowering plants, arranged closely together to create a lush and natural looking field of color. Faeries especially enjoy bell-shaped flowers, which they can play with by tapping them as if ringing a real bell. You'll need to garden organically, because chemically treated plants are said to be avoided by faeries. You may, however, enhance your garden with manmade art. Decorate with faerie statues, faerie furniture, or water features. If you play music in your garden, you will also find faeries flocking to its pleasant ambiance. Attracting local animals by planting butterfly flowers and putting up bird baths and feeders will bring cheerful faeries who love to be around their animal friends.

I don't know about you, but I am a terrible gardener and tend to kill the plants I try to keep. If you can't keep a faerie garden, for whatever reason, but you still want to set something up to attract outdoor faeries, consider building a faerie grotto. If you can build a faerie grotto on your property, start with natural rock features and crystals. If you can, add a fountain, but otherwise you can use a birdbath or an offering bowl of water as a water source. Showing the faeries that the grotto is just for them with statues, faerie furniture, or other art may help. You can make offerings of food or drink nightly to the faeries in the grotto. Since you won't be cultivating plants there, you can still benefit from the faerie-attracting powers of flowers by offering flowers in a vase or strung into a garland.

Evidence of Faeries

How can you tell if faeries have graced your home or garden? The best way to tell that there are faeries making your life more magical is that the space will feel more peaceful and welcoming to you than before you started inviting their presence. In the garden, flowers should bloom more frequently, for a longer duration, and be larger and more colorful when faeries are around. Likewise, you'll see the presence of natural wildlife increase, with more sightings of beautiful birds, butterflies, frogs, dragonflies, lizards, squirrels, and deer or other local fauna. In your home, your housecleaning efforts will seem to last for a longer period of time before the smudges and dust bunnies return. You may even catch the scent of faeries working their magic in your home with the aromas of flowers or sweet baked goods.

Faerie rings are my favorite evidence of their presence. A faerie ring is a circle of toadstools. Some say that faerie rings are portals for faeries to jump between dimensions. Others say that faerie rings are like a circle of chairs used for faerie council meetings or dance parties. I saw many a faerie ring of white toadstools in my front yard when I was a child growing up. Every year, I would find one nearly in the same spot as the spring or fall before, and I would sit in the middle of the three to six foot circle of toadstools, feeling nature's magic. Last year I was delighted to find a faerie ring had appeared in my yard, which awakened old feelings of childhood delight and my early connection with the little people.

Seeing Faeries

Some people see faeries in their mind's eye, in dreams, or in the corners of their actual field of vision. They might appear as the classic winged creatures of faerie tales, or they may be tiny sparkling lights or fleeting shadows caught only for an instant in your mental picture. You may have heard of phenomena like ghosts being caught on camera, and it has been said that faeries might also allow themselves to appear as light effects on photographs. So, if you have never been able to see a faerie, try creating a faerie garden and then take plenty of pictures around your most beautiful flowers and visiting wildlife.

Finding a rock that has a natural hole in the middle is considered a gift from the faeries, a "holey stone." Hold up a holey stone and look through the hole. You may be able to see faeries with your real eyes for the first time. A holey stone has also been said to give people visions of the future, so such a gift from the faeries should be treated with reverence. Keep a holey stone on your elemental altar in the area facing north, or make it into a pendant and wear it as a protective amulet from the faeries.

Of course, there are also magical ways to give yourself faerie sight. Traditionally, magic potions smeared on the eyelids were used to see faeries. There are no surviving recipes of ancient magic potions for faerie sight. It may be that such potions were actually tinctures of hallucinogenic plants. After all, potentially hallucinogenic drinks such as absinthe have always been associated with seeing green faeries. Modern faerie lovers have made countless attempts at the potion using plants that are associated with faeries. For example, it is said that if you find a four-leaf clover and blend it with faerie flowers like hollyhock, marigold, thyme, elecampane, and hazel, the resulting dried flowers steeped in an oil such as grapeseed will make a good substitute. Store the oil in a dark bottle in a cool place. When you want to see faeries, take yourself out in nature at dawn, noon, dusk, or midnight. Smear a bit of the oil on each eyelid, and keep a watchful eye on a field of flowers. If you think you see a faerie, hold your eyes still without moving them and especially without blinking. Allow the faerie to choose to move into your field of vision, otherwise he or she will disappear with a blink.

If you are of the proper age, constitution, and mindset to drink alcohol, using a bit of absinthe is the traditional method for bringing you in touch with the green faerie that is an artistic muse. Grab a friend and a bottle of absinthe that contains real grand wormwood (*Artemisia absinthium*), along with a couple of glasses, some ice, water, sugar cubes, and an absinthe spoon. An absinthe spoon is usually a piece of decorated silverware featuring a large, flat triangle with holes in it at the top. If you can't acquire an absinthe spoon, a large fork or a serving spoon with holes in it will do in a pinch.

Again, go out in nature at dawn, noon, dusk, or midnight. Start by pouring an ounce of absinthe into a serving glass. Mix a little bit of water with your ice so that the ice water slurry is thick with ice. Place a sugar cube on top of the slotted spoon, and hold it over a serving glass. Slowly pour the ice water mixture over the sugar cube until it is completely dissolved. When done correctly, you should see the absinthe become cloudy. Go outside and take a sip. Use the same method of watching for faeries as with the faerie sight potion.

Getting on Their Good Side

Although different faerie types have varying lore as to how they are best appeased, in general faeries are more likely to be on friendly terms with you if you treat them with respect. Treating faeries with respect means offering them food and drink as you would honored guests, but especially entails treating the environment well. Don't litter, do your part to conserve natural resources and energy, recycle, and leave a small carbon footprint. Remember that your home is your environment as well, so pick up things that are left scattered about on the floor. Be sure to dust, sweep, mop, or vacuum.

How to Talk to Faeries

Get out in the natural world and talk aloud to the faeries. The best times of day to get their attention are at dawn, noon, dusk, and midnight, when they are most active. A full moon may get more night faeries flitting about. May and October are the best months to try to first get in touch with faeries. Midsummer, the summer solstice, has traditionally been associated with faerie gatherings. At the end of October, it is said that the veil between worlds becomes thin, so perhaps faeries from other realms can more easily pay a visit to ours.

Get their attention with an offering of something shiny or some sweet food. You can even find a sparkly rock and leave it for the faeries. Remove any non-biodegradable packaging from candy before leaving it outdoors, of course, or they may feel more slighted than treated. Leaving an offering is absolutely vital, or else the light-fingered faeries will simply take an offering that you may not have intended to give. For example, if the faeries desire a shiny trinket, and you did not leave them a sparkly piece of rock candy from your pantry, they might steal your car keys instead, leaving you to look high and low for them.

If you feel moved to do so, faeries respond better if you put your words into song. You can also write a letter and leave it for the faeries, if you're shy about talking out loud to things that you can't see. Faeries love children, so if you have kids, invite them to come and talk to the faeries with you, and the faeries may listen to your kids' request more than your own. You could tell your children to put in a good word for you. In turn, perhaps you can offer to put in a good word with *your* close personal friend, the Tooth Faerie.

How to Get Rid of Faeries

If you find that your home is infested with the nasty and troublesome sort of faerie that is frightening your family, ruining food, or stealing your belongings, you may wish to encourage them to take their leave. This is called "laying" a faerie. Start by simply asking the faeries to leave. Make sure to refer to them as faeries, since some types of faeries disappear when their true nature is called out. If the faeries try to offer you a parting gift, do not accept it. The gift may be a trick to put you in their debt and thus allow them to demand to stay. If the faeries speak to you, whether it be in your dreams or simply in your mind's fancy, always reply in rhyme, since that can banish a faerie, almost like you are having a poetry battle. For faeries that don't speak English, ring a bell around the house, snap your fingers, and clap your hands to frighten them away.

If asking the faeries to leave doesn't work, you should lay a faerie by offering them an entire outfit of clothes. Make or buy a tiny suit of clothes the size for a doll and lay them out at night. Leaving a sock under the bed may work as well. In many myths and legends, faeries pack up and leave immediately upon being offered clothes.

Finally, there are a few ways to ward away faeries once you have gotten them to vacate the premises. You can keep them from following you back home and infesting your home again simply by crossing water. If you feel you might be under magical attack by mischievous faeries, wash your hair with sage and wear a hat and coat inside out to fend off their onslaughts while you set up the defenses. An acorn kept in a pocket and ashes from a midsummer bonfire in your shoes are protective charms as well. Start with salt sprinkled around the home as if it were a wall that keeps them out. Placing a few anti-faerie charms at the entrances of your home will finish the job. Below are a few examples of such charms:

- A four-leaf clover. This lucky charm will flush faeries out, allowing you to both see and be protected against them.

- St. John's Wort flowers and daisies woven into a garland.

- An equal-armed cross of sticks of rowan, oak, ash, or hawthorn, bound with red thread.

- Anything made of iron.

- Ashes and kelp mixed with sea salt (especially effective against water faeries).

- A mulberry tree planted near the door.

Common Faerie Types, Characteristics, Origins, and Where They Are Found

Angels—Air

Though angels are best known in the West from Christian mythology, there is lore that departs from Biblical angels. Some faeries are said to be fallen angels. That is not to say that all angelic faeries are evil once they leave heaven. Yes, some are naughty. But others are seeking to garner favor to gain entry back into heaven, and doing so by helping humans. Others may have been sent down from heaven to do good work on earth.

In ceremonial magic, the archangels Michael, Gabriel, Raphael, and Auriel are powerful beings associated with the planets and the four elemental quarters. Raphael was associated with the planet Mercury, Gabriel with the moon, Michael with the sun, and Auriel with Mars. The names of these archangels are intoned to raise power for magical purposes. You need only speak their names to have them stand at your side for guidance or protection.

Anthropophagi—Air

These faeries made their written debut in folklore described in Shakespeare's plays, although they dwelled around England before his time. They are headless, with eyes sitting on their shoulders and tiny brains that reside in their genitals. Gaping mouths are in their chests. They feed on human flesh and should be avoided at all costs.

Apsaras—Water

The Apsara exists in both Hindu and Buddhist spiritual mythologies. Apsaras can change shape, but their true forms are beautiful young females who are the spirits of water, clouds, and gambling. Apsaras have the power of flight, enjoy dancing, and are good at caring for those who have fallen in battle and require healing.

Apsaras are pleased by music that is good for dancing, as well as by the presence of water. Men should take care not to be seduced by an aspara, for according to mythology their hearts will be broken and their minds made numb to the world's spiritual ideals. Since aspara love to dance so much, they are also honored in it, and have inspired a Khmer dance, *Robam*

Tep Apsara ("dance of the Apsara divinities"), performed by the Royal Ballet of Cambodia.

Ashrays—Water

In Scotland are beautiful young sea creatures called ashrays, which look like the translucent white ghosts of humans. They are not ghosts, however, but living creatures that dwell in the sea. Their white skin may be due to the fact that they can never see the light of day; sunlight melts them, rendering them into pools of water the colors of the rainbow.

Like any other sea creature, ashrays are most pleased by humans reducing their impact on their watery environment. Unfortunately, you're unlikely to make contact with them, as they live deep underwater and generally avoid humans.

Attorcroppes—Earth

From Saxony, the attorcroppe is a snake with arms and legs that walks just like a human. It is very small, as many faerie creatures are, but vicious and venomous. They live among rocky areas, especially near wilderness and water. To keep clear of them, one should avoid walking along rocky stream beds at night.

Ballybogs, Bogles, Boggans—Earth

Widespread throughout England, Ireland, Wales, and the Isle of Man, ballybogs are also known as bogles and boggans regionally. Small, round and mud-covered, ballybogs have tiny arms and legs that don't seem to support their weight. The slimmer English variant, boggans, are the only ones to wear clothes and to be intelligent enough for speech. The vast majority of bally-bogs communicate only in short grunts.

Ballybogs are found near bogs, and they would delight in gifts of peat and peaty alcoholic drinks. Some of their favorite games are footraces and tag. A ballybog can be requested for help finding anything that has been lost in a boggy area, but they do so by physically running to show you, since they are unlikely to be able to communicate to you in words.

Ban-Tighes—Earth

Not to be confused with banshees, ban-tees are female house faeries. Often seen as elderly women, they are so friendly to people that they bond to a house or a family, and stay for generations to protect and help around the house. Ban-tees are especially fond of homes with children or pets, and they love to look after them and tidy up when messes occur.

To make contact with a ban-tee, leave out strawberries and cream as an offering near the hearth during the late fall, winter, and early spring whenever you are too tired to finish your household drudgery. You will know that your gift has been accepted if the chores are finished in the morning, or if you notice somebody making sure that the windows, curtains, and blankets are adjusted to keep children and pets warm.

Basilisk—Fire

A basilisk is a real lizard, but the word also refers to a mythological faerie creature from Greece. The mythological basilisk is a snake with arms gleaming gold and a bright red spiky or frilly comb on the top of its head. Basilisks are vicious and venomous, and can spread their venom simply by breathing upon, touching, or looking at a human being. Even killing a basilisk is dangerous in and of itself, since the body is filled with its poisonous breath. The good news is that they don't reproduce quickly. Supposedly, basilisk eggs are laid by roosters and incubated for nine years by toads.

To keep a basilisk at bay, you need only have its natural enemies living in the area: crows, mongooses, roosters, snakes, or weasels. Mirrors can also protect the wanderer from a basilisk, since they can be warded off or possibly even destroyed simply by viewing their own reflections.

Bean Fionns, Greentoothed Women, Jenny Greenteeth, Weisse Fraus—Water

A bean fionn can be found in bodies of water mainly in England, Germany, and Ireland. Though a kiss from this water faerie can render anyone immune to drowning, they are temperamental and as likely to kill a traveler as protect him or her. A bean fionn is the personification of the fear of one's children being drowned. Nightmarishly, the faeries will reach up from below the water and grab children playing in water or even close to the shore or on a bridge.

These most dangerous of water faeries are most likely to be found in the darkest of lakes, which should be avoided at all costs. Charms against drowning, like an amulet made from a bag of ashes, kelp, and sea salt, may keep away their attacks.

Beansidhes, Cointeach, Cyoerraeth, Washer at the Banks/Fords (of Shrouds)—Water

Sometimes spelled as "banshees," these terrors announce or portend death with blood-curdling wails, and are originally from Ireland, Scotland, England, and Wales. In Scotland, a similar male variant also exists called a Ly Erg, who appears as a small soldier with a red hand. If he raises his hand to you, it is to challenge you to combat as a way of foretelling your death.

Always female, banshees appear as winged human women, but they are faeries that are sometimes mistaken for ghosts. Banshees appear beside rivers or streams, most often seen washing burial shrouds and keening in grief. They are a normal human size. Banshees are pale, have long hair that appears wet, and are often depicted wearing a white, green, or black gown with a hood that obscures the hair or face. If you see her open her mouth to wail, her teeth will be pitch black.

Banshees are only scary because their wailing foretells of a death, and upon hearing a banshee a person cannot help but wonder if it is oneself or one's loved ones that are to die. The banshees themselves are not dangerous, and may represent a mother form who absorbs a soul before rebirth. You should probably be very afraid if one shows up at your door or window flapping her wings, but otherwise she should be left to mourn in peace.

Black Anguses—Water

From England and Scotland, a black angus is a creature that is not humanoid, but instead looks like a horned black dog with huge fangs, wet paws, and gleaming yellow eyes. Like banshees, black anguses are not dangerous themselves, but their howling portends a terrible or violent death, especially for those who have done such dark deeds as to expect to have a miserable time in the afterlife.

If a black angus crosses your path at night and leaps in front of you, be afraid that you might die within two weeks. Otherwise, have no fear of this dog faerie passing in the night. Just be relieved in the same way that you might be glad that a passing ambulance is not coming for you. Don't attempt communication with a black angus—you wouldn't want to tempt fate.

Blue Hag, Black Annis, Cailleach Bheare, Stone Woman—Water

There is only one Blue Hag, but she is widespread, like a goddess figure, throughout Celtic lands. She appears to be an old woman in blue (or black) and white torn clothing, with a crow on her left shoulder. She goes out walking on winter nights, and may be temperamental and dangerous. She carries a walking stick made of holly and with the head of a crow at its top. If you were to be touched by her walking stick, you could die. She may be the embodiment of the crone aspect of female divinity, and should be respected as a goddess, if not feared.

Bocans—Air

Bocans are terrifying creatures that robbed and killed people in medieval times. It was not a good idea to travel at night, because on the highways between towns, bocans might be lying in wait. Since nobody ever lived through a bocan attack, there are no physical descriptions of the creatures. Though they were rare even in their heyday, the best way to prevent an encounter was simply to restrict travel to daylight hours and to journey together in large groups.

Boggart, Boogey Men, Goblins, Hobgoblins—Earth

A Scottish or English dwarf creature, a boggart is always male. Boggarts are malicious creatures, but are drawn to keep company with humans for some strange reason. Boggarts will choose a household or a family and stick around for generations, plaguing them with grumpy interactions and greedy thievery of food and belongings. Especially frightening to children, boggarts can jump upon them at night so that the child feels like he or she is being smothered to death.

Like vermin, the boggart chews through objects and destroys them. Wood is a favorite treat, and a boggart can consume pieces of valuable furniture or even the floors and walls of the home itself. Due to their voracious appetites, leaving out wood as an offering will not be enough to satiate their destructive desires.

In the wild, boggarts may have lived in bogs, so the best way to avoid a boggart may simply be to avoid building or buying a home at the side of a bog. If a boggart does take up residence, they are especially stubborn, and it may take more than one attempt to rid your home of malicious boggart activity.

Brown Men, Moor Men—Fire

Originating from Cornwall or Scotland, brown men are not actually brown. Their hair is reddish, and it is the torn clothes they wear that are brown, as they are made from leaves that have become wet and rotted in the rain. Brown men are short, always male, and have long arms that are quite fat.

Brown men tend not to meddle in the affairs of humans. If you call out to them near a moor, chances are that they will shy away from you. Brown men are quite harmless; they keep their distance and live only in wild places.

Brownies, Choa Phum Phi, Domovoi, Hobs, Little Men, Nis, Yumboes—Earth

Brownies are from Scotland, originally. They are small and normally do not allow themselves to be seen. If you do catch sight of a brownie, he (brownies are usually male) will generally be naked and hairy, or only wearing tattered brown wool. They do not have noses. Two holes in the face mark where a nose should be. They also have no fingers or toes at the ends of their furry arms and legs. Add the fact that they are often seen with tails, and they are strange creatures indeed.

Making friends with brownies can be rewarding, because they help around the house. Brownies tend to befriend a family and stick with it through generations. They can ward the house from trouble, assisting you in calling for help if something goes wrong, making them a bit like a mythical neighborhood watch. They can also do chores around the house gladly and happily, banding together to get a whole day's work done in a very short time during the night. If you make your brownies unhappy, however, you'll find yourself saddled with terrible luck as they begin to cause trouble in subtle ways.

Brownies only work at night, after all of the members of the household have gone to sleep. Having house brownies is sort of like having pets, in that food and drink should be offered nightly to them. Only a tiny, token amount need be set out. Offerings that brownies are pleased to accept are bowls of cream and a pancake with honey on top. Like the pixies, brownies will leave a home forever if the owner offers an article of clothing. In fact, no other offering but food and drink should be given to brownies, and they should not be spoken of aloud in the house. It is said that brownies will stop working to listen to you talk about them, becoming suspicious and nervous, and hearing criticism even when you are not criticizing them at all. If a brownie thinks that it is not being appreciated, it will fly into a rage and leave, never to help again. Unlike pixies, brownies can often be industrious and helpful, and should be cared for as welcome family heirlooms.

Buachailleen, Herding Boys—Earth

Buachailleen hail from both Ireland and Scotland. There, they are known for playing mean pranks on people and animals. Buachailleen look like little boys with pointed hats made from overturned red flowers. However, they can shapeshift to whatever form they desire on a whim, and usually do so to make mischief.

The normal target of buachailleen torment is a shepherd and his flock. Buachailleen boys will do anything to frighten the animals, lead them astray, and generally be cruel. When herding sheep in the areas infested with buachailleen, one would do well to pray and chant aloud for protection of the flocks.

Bugel Noz—Earth

Rather than a race of creatures, the Bugel Noz is an individual faerie person in Brittany. Though he lives by himself in the woods, he is very lonely, being the last of his species. Sadly, he is so ugly and terrifying in appearance that humans and animals run from him. Bugel Noz may have to live out an immortal or mysteriously long life in solitude. However, he calls out to those who walk in the forest to warn them of his appearance before he emerges. Since Bugel Noz is harmless, it is fine to stand your ground and see if you can be his first friend, should your paths ever cross.

Buggars—Air

Coming from England and Germany, buggars are thought to be either a type of troll or goblin. They tend to shapeshift so frequently that they have never been accurately described. Buggars act very much like violent toddlers having tantrums, but when they take a larger form, they are far more dangerous. Buggars are to be avoided, but luckily they stay out of the human physical world as much as possible, for the most part only making an appearance to scare children.

Bunyips—Water

Bunyips come from wetland regions of the land down under, but may have also originated in central Africa as well as Australia. They are about four feet in height, and are fat and humanoid with feet turned backwards. Bunyips are coated with a thick layer of the muck and the mire of the swamp.

Friendly bunyips are helpful to humans, warning of danger, leading hunters to prey, and chasing away dangerous wildlife. A bunyip emerges at night or during the crepuscular hour, but legends say that only those of aboriginal origin may be able to actually see their physical forms. Bunyips make a sound that is very much like a dog barking.

You can call out to a bunyip for assistance, should you ever find yourself wandering in a swampy region of Australia. Even if you cannot see the bunyips, listen for their barking to allow them to lead you or warn you during your travels.

Bwaganods—Water

Welsh goblins called bwaganods spend most of their time occupying a humanoid shape, but can shapeshift to anything they like. Luckily for people, bwaganods are terribly sloppy shapeshifters, and usually make a mistake that leaves their form so outlandish as to be clearly identified as a bwaganod. Bwaganods emerge at dusk and enjoy frightening humans for fun and because they dislike them. Avoiding a bwaganod is easy, since they are largely harmless and the fun stops for them when their prank is discovered.

Bwciods—Fire

Bwciods are solitary Welsh goblins that are a foot tall in height. They are skinny and have enormous feet. Their hands are slender and long, and their noses are pointy. All bwciods have purple eyes and emotionless faces that don't show their feelings. Their faces are deceptive, since they can be quick to anger and can be dangerous or annoying when provoked.

At night, bwciods wander in wilderness places looking for humans to follow home. Though they don't necessarily like interacting with people, they do love peoples' homes. When your house becomes occupied by a bwciod, it is very difficult to make him or her leave. The best way to prevent a bwciod infestation is to make sure that one doesn't follow you home. The charms listed on page 19 may help!

Callicantzaroi—Earth

From Albania, Greece, and Italy, callicantzaroi are naked faeries that are small and thin, each with the feet of a different wild animal. They travel in groups during the winter, riding atop chickens and wearing fantastic and fancy hats. Callicantzaroi are functionally blind and mostly harmless. However, callicantzaroi pollute the water they use, so if you have callicantzaroi around your water sources, you are advised to add a bit of hyssop to magically counteract their effect. It is said that lighting an old shoe on fire and setting it outside will scare the callicantzaroi away for good if you don't want them around. If you want to get to know or like them, give them an offering of pork.

Changelings—Earth

Originating in European folklore, a changeling is an elf or a troll that has been switched with a human baby shortly after birth so that the human family would raise it as their own. Faeries of all types were blamed with the theft of children. After all, in ancient times, childhood diseases were rampant and many children did not live to adulthood. Perhaps mythology about changelings helped parents come to terms with an early death or come to grips with the mysterious and terrifying effects of a childhood disease. Scariest of all, a changeling child that did live would often suddenly disappear, running away to rejoin his or her own faerie family.

Changeling children could be recognized by their striking good looks, and they were often described as having golden hair. Despite their physical beauty, changeling children were always of delicate health. The only way to cure a changeling or to prevent a child from being switched with a changeling was baptism in water.

Chi Spirits—Air

Chinese chi spirits are called spirits because they have no physical form—they manifest in the air as pure spiritual energy. Though they are invisible, they do establish residence in the physical homes of humans, adopting a household or family for generations. It is thought that chi spirits may be helpful (or even necessary) to help a family's day-to-day life run smoothly and efficiently.

Chi spirits strongly dislike their way being blocked, so cluttered rooms may cause them to be unable to help their humans. When chi spirits are blocked, they can cause illness, bad luck, or disorder. Ask the chi spirits of your home for guidance and to be inspired when tidying up or redecorating.

Chin-Chin Kobakamas—Earth

Originating from Japan, chin-chin kobakamas are agile house elves which are elderly in appearance, and they are attracted in particular to human rugs. They are friendly toward humans, but not terribly helpful around the house. Instead, they tease and cause mischief if one is a terrible housekeeper, encouragement for a person to get chores done. To please the chin-chin kobakamas, one need only make sure to keep a tidy house.

Cottagers/Booakers/Bwbachs—Earth

The Welsh faeries called cottagers are always male, small, and rotund, and wear fur cloaks, loincloths that look like diapers, and big red hats. They prefer to live in the homes of humans, but having cottagers around is a mixed bag. Though they are great guardians of homes, frightening off intruders, they tend to mistake friends of the household as intruders. If your home is infested with cottagers, you might offer them cake with milk for distraction when guests come calling.

Cucuis—Earth

Migrating from Mexico to America with Hispanic communities, cucuis are monsters that look like ghouls or zombies with wide, empty eyes and a drooling maw. Like zombies in popular culture, cucuis seem brainless and live only to pursue humans to hurt or destroy them. Luckily, a cucui is not very intelligent; they can be easily outwitted and eluded.

Devas—Earth

Though devas became famous at a place called Findhorn in Scotland, they can be found anywhere in the world and may have originated in Persia. Devas are very small creatures, often invisible to the naked eye, but identifiable in photographs as balls of light. Some believe that they are golden faeries with brightly colored robes, if you were able to see through their bright orbs of light. A deva's main goal is to help plants grow, so they are vital to having healthy crops or a prize-winning garden. Every plant process is guided by devas, from germination of the seeds to flowering and production of fruit and even the death of the plant. Though devas' main concern is with plants, they can also help with weather magic, animals, or even human health and beauty.

Devas can be thought of as operating on a microscopic, molecular level. They embody the energetic force that makes life proceed as normal. They are the personification of atomic forces. As such, there may be different devas for each category of living thing as well as subcategories within them, down to the level of species or even individuals. Devas can actually evolve and change over the lifetime of the creature or plant that they serve, within its life cycle or within the food chain. So, if a carrot deva is consumed by a rabbit deva, it too becomes a rabbit deva.

Some gardeners spend much of their gardening time pleasing devas with songs and offerings. The best way to establish a relationship with devas is simply to remain mindful and aware of their presence and existence. Much like the silly part of *Peter Pan* in which the character Tinker Bell is sustained by people who believe in faeries, devas thrive on the concept of belief. It is as if devas feed off the energy of humans who spend time in meditation or think about the nature of the universe. Of course, such mindfulness only benefits the humans, without taking anything away from them. In return, devas can help the plants directly, and also impart knowledge and teachings through dreams or inspiration during meditation. So if after singing to your plants you have a niggling notion in your mind about how to help them grow bigger and better, it just might be a nudge from the devas.

Just as devas evolve along the food chain or life cycle of living things, their nature can be influenced by humans. Devas in a garden that is deeply loved and served by its human caretakers might then evolve from being merely turnip devas, for example, into devas of the spirit of gardening. By serving devas, we may be assisting them to reach their highest spiritual potential, just as they help us with our greatest passions in life, in a sort of symbiotic spiritual relationship.

Dinnshenchas—Fire

Servants of the goddess Aine, dinnshenchas are Irish dwarf faeries. They can shapeshift to any form that they wish, so don't expect them to necessarily appear as stereotypical dwarves or faeries. Dinnshenchas are dedicated to the protection of women, due to their service to a goddess who was the survivor of rape. Women can call upon the guardian help of dinnshenchas during any time of need when they are being wronged. Dinnshenchas can take on terrifying forms to protect women from attackers.

Dracs, Dracae, Nix—Water

Found in France, England, and Germany, dracs are giant, floating purple blobs that usually appear on or near water. Dracs can shapeshift into the form of a golden chalice or a woman. Dracs frolic near natural bodies of water, or even just in damp forests. They enjoy floating down rivers on wooden rafts that look like plates. Dracs are harmless when you keep your distance, but are not helpful. They may devour or kidnap men when they reach toward the water to claim their prize. At that moment, the drac will grab the man and drag him away to either drown or live in captivity below the water.

Drakes—Fire

Originating in England, drakes are house faeries that seek out human homes that have a fireplace and a welcoming family. Though invisible to the eye, drakes have a very strong sulfurous smell that is not terribly pleasant. However, the services drakes provide are worth the terrible smell, since they keep firewood dry and help the hearth fire start and keep burning through the night.

Drakes enjoy offerings of food and old wood, and are more likely to take up residence in a home that is out in the country or near a forest. If offerings are withheld, a drake may become upset and leave the home forever.

Duckfeet/Erdluitles—Earth

The males of these Swiss dwarf faeries are called Hardmandlene, while the females are called Erdbiberli. Though they do have webbed feet, they can't swim and they keep their feet hidden by wearing long, hooded cloaks. A duckfoot has magical control over the weather, but as they are shy around humans, they are unlikely to offer help with the weather to just anyone. In the past, farmers were able to gain the favor of a duckfoot by being polite. Pleasant weather would follow, helping the crops to ripen.

Duendes—Earth

Though duendes appeared first in Spain, they migrated with the Spanish people to the Americas. Duendes always appear as small women with long and slender fingers that taper to a point. They wear green robes and live solitary lives. Duendes are extremely envious and possessive, and especially like to try to take over a human home and drive its human occupants away.

Though they do tidy up the houses they infest since they like order in their environment, make no mistake, they are not trying to help. A duende will set about creating cruel practical jokes, moving furniture, and tossing and breaking objects in the home. Things can get quite dangerous if a duende starts throwing cutlery. The best course of action if your home becomes infested is to evict her. Any attempt to placate her will only make her envious about what resources you have that she does not.

Duergaars—Earth

These dwarf faeries may be from England, France, and Spain. Appearing as nearly two-foot-tall people wearing clothes of moleskin and green hats, they are ill-tempered and unfriendly to humans. Duergaars live solitary lives, usually setting up residence on a faerie path in the woods. Since they dislike humans, a duergaar will viciously guard his or her path in the woods and will work to steer humans away or make them lose their way in the forest. Duergaars tamper with human trail markers to confuse and disorient travelers.

Dybbukkim, Lobs—Air

Dybbukkim are Jewish spirits that are demonic in nature. They are invisible, but can possess people to take the form of human bodies. A similar creature, the Lob, that may have originally come from either Wales, Germany, or England, is said to take the form of a dark cloud with arms. A dybbuk will travel through the air in search of loud human arguments or fights. Feeding off the energy of discord, the dybbuk waits until a human has become vulnerable through acts of evil or violence. When a human has become spiritually weakened, the dybbuk will possess him or her to have a tangible form.

Dybbukkim are never helpful. They are always harmful, especially since they halt any recovery from spiritual afflictions. A dybbuk can be exorcised by a rabbi once it has entered a body, or dybukkim can be warded off altogether with music. Even a few musical notes will send a dybbuk flying away to find somewhere else to feed. Consequently, when the atmosphere has turned negative, turn on some music to keep the situation from getting much worse.

Ellyllons—Water

From the lakes of Cornwall and Wales, ellyllons are faeries small enough to ride upon eggshells over the water. Though they live at the bottom of lakes, they cannot be seen when they are below the water's surface. Ellyllons are most commonly spotted during the spring, but they have little interest in either helping or harming humans unless they are worshipers of the lake goddess embodied by the fables of the Lady of the Lake from Arthurian legend.

Erlkonig, Ellerkonge—Air

Erlkonigs are solitary elf kings. In fact, there may be only one since only one has been seen at a time. Though Erlkonig's appearances have occurred in Denmark and Germany, he is said to live in Valhalla when not making brief visits to foretell a death.

The Erlkonig appears only to a person who will die. He wears a crown of gold and other finery. If he looks miserable and suffering, the nature of the death will be horrible. If he looks peaceful and jolly, the death will be just as peaceful.

Farm Faeries, Fireesin, Harvesters—Earth

Farm faeries are ugly, naked, and covered with sparse brown fur. They live a solitary life, seeking out farms for their homes. Once a farm has been found, a farm faerie will take up residence and attempt to help out with the farm chores. Unfortunately, farm faeries are not very intelligent, and the farm faerie's attempts to help might just end up breaking things or making a mess. Farm faeries hibernate during the winter, but tend to cause frustration on farms the rest of the year.

If a farm faerie is banished from a farm, it will become angry and usually destroy crops and livestock as it leaves. So it is best to put up with the minor annoyances of poorly done chores than to evict a farm faerie by offering him or her clothing. After all, once one farm faerie is gone, another one may move right back in.

Fays, Fae, Fadas, Fas, Fatas, Fee—Air

Though from Albania, these faeries may have been named after the Latin word for "fate." They are small and of four distinct types, one for each season. Their appearances are evocative of the seasons; they also help to color and open flowers in the spring, ripen fruit in the summer, make leaves fall in the autumn, and paint frost on the windows in the winter.

Dancing with the fays is the best way to please them, although they are more likely to be caught up in their own important work than to actually help your life. Though they are tangentially associated with the weather of the seasons, they only bring about the inevitable, and so they cannot be asked to work specific weather magic for you.

Fin Folk/the Lady's Own/Sea Gardeners—Water

From Cornwall, Scotland, and Wales, fin folk look like humans, but exist in an underwater kingdom surrounded by a bubble of glass. Fin folk love to garden the watery beds of their domain and enjoy helping fish and other water animals thrive. Though fin folk can breathe air, they never leave their underwater kingdoms, preferring to stay home. They are shy around humans and have shunned the world of dry land, so they are unlikely to invite you to visit unless you commit yourself to helping underwater plants and animals thrive as much as they do.

Formors/Formorians—Water

The formors may have once been humanoid Irish faerie folk. However, they have long since been banished to the sea and turned into frightening sea monsters. The formors can be recognized because they look like many animal parts sewn together. They live in the sea, but can crawl awkwardly upon the shore at nighttime. They are not very intelligent and are quick to anger. The formors can be easily avoided by not going to the seashore or into the sea at night.

Fossegrim—Water

These Norwegian spirits of waterfalls are playful pranksters, but don't truly wish humans either help or harm. They appear to be human themselves, only their lower bodies and feet gradually taper and disappear into mist as if they were the bottoms of waterfalls themselves. Fossegrim enjoy taking the form of particularly attractive humans, even though they don't have any gender differences themselves. In fact, they can switch between male and female human forms to properly trick whatever gender approaches their waterfall homes. Though fossegrim are not cruel, it would be wise to avoid becoming too attached to them, since they only want to toy with people's hearts.

Fylgiar—Air

In Iceland, some people, especially those born with a caul over their head (a leftover layer of membrane from the mother's womb) will have a faerie companion throughout life called a fylgiar. The fylgiar helps its chosen person throughout his or her entire life, and perhaps even for some time after a given lifespan. Fylgiars remain invisible until shortly before their human's death, when they make an appearance to warn of the upcoming demise. If the fylgiar appears as a beautiful and serene faerie, death will be peaceful. If a fylgiar appears mangled and in pain, the death of its human will be a terribly painful one.

If one has been blessed with a fylgiar, one must serve the fylgiar throughout life in return for the fylgiar's service. Serving a fylgiar can be done in dreams, or during meditation when the fylgiar can give specific instructions for how it would like to be helped. This reciprocal relationship helps build a bond of trust that can last beyond death.

Ganconer, Gancanagh—Air

From Cornwall, Ireland, and Scotland, the ganconer faerie is only male. Ganconers are solitary and appear as attractive human men who carry pipes. Strangely enough, a ganconer never smokes his pipe, but only seems to hold it for decorative purposes since he hates the smell of smoke. Ganconers are not friendly to humans, and they exist only to try to steal the hearts of lonely human women. Ganconers do not return love, but allow the strong feelings to consume each woman until she dies.

Ganconers should be avoided, especially by women who are prone to falling for attractive men. If you see a man with a pipe who is not smoking, especially if he is waiting in the forest all alone, walk the other way.

Gandharvas—Earth

Indian faeries called gandharvas serve deities through music and dance. Gandharvas are extremely small and live entirely underground. They are very shy and rarely emerge, though they are harmless to humans if they do. In order to attract gandharvas, one need only make music and dance in praise of the Hindu deities that they serve.

Gans—Air

Gans are faeries that live in the mountains and wild places of the southwestern United States. Apache people used to honor them to avoid accidents or attacks by wild animals when they went out to explore or hunt. Gans are very friendly and helpful, but they require a lot of honor and ritual before they will choose to help humans at all. They may have shared the appearance of the ritual dress the Apache used, which involved white robes, black masks, and headdresses made of wood. To ask for protection from the gans, you can dress yourself in similar attire. Dance to raise energy in praise and service to the gans, and ask for them to help you in return.

Geancanach—Fire

These hearth fire faeries from Ireland and Scotland are very small, just a few inches in height, with pointy ears and eyes that curve upward to a point. Though they are winged, they are never seen in flight. Instead, they seem to magically transport themselves by disappearing and reappearing. Perhaps they fly so fast that they can't be seen, or perhaps they teleport themselves. Light seems to flicker when they move, making them seem like fireflies.

Geancanach love human hearth fires and will be attracted to the warmth of the fire when it is kindled. Though geancanach are not malicious, they aren't very helpful and like to play practical jokes on humans. To avoid their mischief, set out an offering of fresh milk by the hearth fire for the geancanach to drink.

Ghillie Dhu—Fire

The name *ghillie dhu* in their native Scottish Gaelic means "dark shoe." Ghillie dhu are forest spirits that mimic the form of trees, so they look like trees that have an oddly humanoid form. Ghillie dhu are not friendly toward humans and keep to their own in their forests.

Don't tread in a forest in which people have been known to disappear. It may be that a ghillie dhu grabbed them with its long, branch-like fingers and stole them away to a faerie land to work as slaves to the faeries for the rest of their days.

Gianes—Earth

Though gianes may have originated in Italy, they can be found all over Europe. They look like elves dressed in peasant clothing and pointy hats of animal skins. They carry spinning wheel spindles in their back pockets and live solitary lives. Gianes spend most of their time spinning, weaving, and telling fortunes. They are friendly to humans.

To seek your fortune from a giane, go out to the woods at night and ask for your future to be revealed. Beware that gianes don't pull any punches, and may give you harsh news along with the good. If you make friends with a giane, you may be given a piece of woven cloth. Keep it with you, as it will bring you good fortune.

Giants—Air

Giants appear in myths and legends the world over. They most often look like humans (especially ugly ones) of a fantastic size. Since there are so many different kinds of giants, some may be friendly while others are unfriendly due to a distrust of humans who tend to persecute and steal from them. Giants keep to themselves out in the country and mostly live solitary lives. If you want to frighten a giant away from an area, they may be fearful of cats.

Glaistigs—Water

Scottish glaistigs are solitary and territorial, living in the country near farms. The glaistig is a shapeshifter who takes on the form of a woman, but always accidentally applies horse or goat parts to her body. Glaistigs hate men, and will kill them to suck out all their blood for sustenance.

It may be that glaistigs are friendly to other members of the farming family, such as women, or even children or the elderly of either gender. They can be asked for help with the crops, but men should avoid them at all costs, even if they are not attracted to the glaistig's female form.

Golem—Earth

The Jewish golem is a creature created by a magical practitioner for a specific purpose. It is a thoughtform, rather than a sentient entity with which one can interact. Golems may take many forms, but they can be recognized by the vacant stare of something that has no mind of its own. Golems are harmless unless they have been created to harm, in which case they can be killed like a living thing, but without guilt, since they are essentially objects. In some tales, the Hebrew word *emet* ("truth") would be written on the golem's forehead to bring it to life. To destroy it, one would erase the aleph character to make the word *met*, which means "dead."

Grants—Fire

Grants are solitary faerie creatures that associate themselves with a single English town. They appear to be very small horses, but are so oddly shaped that they are eerie to those who look upon them. Though their grotesque deformity frightens people, they are actually quite friendly and want to protect humans from harm.

Whenever any marauders are about to besiege a town that is looked after by a grant, the grant runs through the streets stirring up all of the animals, causing the dogs to bark and the horses to whinny. If you hear the commotion caused by a grant, you can be sure that a group of people who may not wish your town well are on their way.

Gremlins, Gremlers, Sky Boogies—Air

Gremlin is actually the name for a male gremlin. The females are called fifenellas and their babies are widgets. Gremlins come from Germany but have spread all over Europe, and England in particular has many tales about them. Many gremlins are small, but some are almost as large as humans. They are brown-furred with short, pointed ears and mischievous smiles.

Gremlins, as a species, may once have flown with wings, but are no longer winged or capable of flight. As a result, they take out their frustration by destroying airplanes. Gremlins can start fires, pull wires, chew through metal, and cause all manner of destruction. Spandules are a special type of gremlin that enjoy putting ice on the wings of planes, even when temperatures are well above freezing, to cause fatal crashes. There is no known way to appease a gremlin except to abandon an airplane to its destruction.

Griffins/Griffiths/Geetoes/Gittos/Gryphons—Air

These legendary creatures usually have the head and wings of an eagle and the body of a lion. Welsh griffins are a bit different, having the body of a goat with the head of a horse—and they can float through the air and have the magical power to cause crops to die. They are most active in the fall and winter. Griffins have human voices and the power of speech, but they are very unfriendly and will not hold pleasant conversation.

Griffins do not like people, but often a satisfactory arrangement can be made between people and griffins. The people leave some of the crops in the fields after the final harvest on Halloween so that the griffins can eat or destroy them. That way, hopefully the rest of the gathered harvest will be spared.

Guriuz—Air

Guriuz are creatures from Italy that look like elves. They have the ability to control the weather, so keeping on their good side is of great interest to farmers. Though the guriuz may hibernate during the winter, they are friendly toward those who raise plants from the earth during the rest of the year.

Gwragedd Annwn—Water

Female water faeries called gwragedd annwn come from Wales and are guardians of children, mothers, and the poor. Gwragedd annwn appear as breathtakingly beautiful human women, but they normally make their home at the bottom of mountain lakes. When they do emerge, they are very friendly to humans. Gwragedd annwn are always patient and loving with human children, but may be a bit moody and quick to cause drama in mixed social settings. They love the number five and collect objects from the lake in that number. In fact, they cannot count higher than the number five.

Gwragedd annwn can be approached gladly, although you may have to be overly polite so as not to offend them. They enjoy music and dancing, if you would like to make them happy. Men can fall in love with and even marry gwragedd annwn without it ending in strife as with many other faerie marriages. Humans and gwragedd annwn can interbreed to make beautiful children who love music.

Gwyllions—Fire

These faeries may once have been able to fly, but they no longer have the power of flight. They guard the wild mountain goats of Wales, and only come out at night. They mostly keep to themselves and are so very rarely seen that it may be hard to find a reliable description of them, since they are normally spoken of as strange figures seen in the mountains at night.

Gwyllions are not unfriendly toward humans, only shy. They fear storms, and so a friendship can be made with them if you offer them shelter in the rain. Never threaten a gwyllion, especially with a knife. Though a gwyllion is said to grant a wish when frightened by a knife, he or she may spend a lifetime getting even with the human who made such a threat.

Herdswomen, Firesitters, Gruagachs—Earth

A herdswoman is a faerie woman that looks like a human, only she is quite old and deformed. Wandering Scotland, carrying a shepherd's crook and wearing a gown of green or gold, a herdswoman seeks out companionship and a warm fire. When meeting humans, they normally shun her because of her ugliness, so she is always lonely and cold. Even when she does find somebody to speak with, they normally ignore her because her attention span is too short to be able to understand long stories.

If you meet a herdswoman, invite her to sit by the fire. She will be so overjoyed to have good conversation and warmth that she will gladly help you. She helps cattle find water and stay out of trouble, and guards livestock from malevolent faeries. Offering a herdswoman some milk will also please her.

His Nibs, Clurichauns, Monciellos—Earth

Found in both Italy and Ireland, his nibs are solitary faerie creatures that are short, wingless, elderly, and male, wearing red hats made of flowers. His nibs find and then guard wine cellars, so that they can drink far too much themselves. His nibs are cheerful drunks, however. Even though they take wine for themselves, they also prevent cask leakage and stop the wines from turning to vinegar. They gladly allow the owner of the cellar to take as much as he or she wants, but chase away would-be wine thieves that are not his nibs themselves.

The trouble with his nibs is that they require polite hospitality. Leave out wine for his nibs to drink, otherwise they may become upset by your rudeness and destroy your entire stock of wine before leaving forever.

Houris—Air

Houris are spiritual creatures of Arabic origin that represent the ecstasy of the awareness of God. Described as being attractive men or women, each endowed with translucent skin and an especially arresting gaze, houris are very tall creatures with no hair except on their heads. Houris have few biological needs, as they don't eat or defecate. Even gestation lasts only an hour for them, without showing any sign of the pregnancy.

As a result, a houri cannot be lured by food like other beings. Instead, as pure creatures that belong to God, a houri may be attracted, or come into being, due to a good deed. In fact, houris may be the pure physical manifestation of good deeds pleasing to God.

Howlers, Glashtin, Hawlaa, Howlies—Air

On the Isle of Man and perhaps in Scotland, these faeries appear to be half cow and half horse, though which animal has the head and which has the tail may vary. Those with the head of a horse are smart while those with the head of a cow are dull.

Howlers are so named because they howl with joy before a storm appears. The howlers can be a good warning before an especially destructive windstorm. They enjoy riding on the wind and laughing as the wind causes property damage. It is possible that howlers even cause such storms. There is no way to prevent a storm caused or heralded by a howler, but you can take cover.

Hyldermolders—Earth

Scandinavian hyldermolders have spread all over Europe to guard the sacred elder tree. Hyldermolders are always female, and appear as elderly matriarchs in beautiful green gowns. A hyldermolder can be asked during the full moon to work mother goddess magic. Anything to do with fertility, abundance, or psychic power is easily granted by her magic. However, never try to steal wood from the elder tree by cutting or burning it, or you will find that she can attack with malice and frightening magic.

Hysters—Air

Hysters may have originated in Spain or England and spread all over the world, and they are shapeshifters that normally take the form of birds. They like to frighten humans, so they'll pick a bird that makes a person uneasy, like a buzzard or a vulture, and may even wear a human face. A hyster's idea of a good time is to dive-bomb a human to frighten him or her. Though they are not dangerous, hysters are also not helpful.

Ieles—Earth

The terrifying ileles of Eastern Europe wait near human paths at night. They look like big cats that walk on their hind legs. They attack and kill humans and suck their blood. If you see an ilele, he or she may try to lure you away from a busy road by dancing or making beautiful music. Do not follow an ilele. Instead, retreat to a crossroads. Ileles cannot enter crossroads, as the magical intersections take away their power.

Jinn, Afreets, Djinn, Genies, Jinnis, Jeenies—Air

From Persia and Saudi Arabia, these spirits live inside magical receptacles. Female jinn live in bottles while male jinn live inside oil lamps. When the magical receptacle is rubbed by a human, the jinn will emerge and offer to do the bidding of the human. However, jinn are not naturally very friendly, and they may try to trick the very people that they serve.

Kelpies, Fuath, Nickers, Nuggies, Shoneys, Uisges—Water

From Cornwall, Ireland, Scotland, Norway, Germany, Shetland, and other regions, kelpies are small and round. With webbed feet, horse's tails, pointed ears, and large teeth, kelpies may be funny to look at, but they are easily given to rage and somehow manage to be both sneaky and simple.

When left in the wild, kelpies live near the water and feed on wild deer. They may try to lure humans toward the water to eat them. Kelpies can shapeshift, but do so poorly, leaving seaweed on their person as a dead giveaway. If you see a kelpie taking the form of a seahorse or a beautiful human with seaweed hair, stay away from the water.

Knockers, Black Dwarves, Coblynaus, Gommes, Paras, Wichlein—Earth

Knockers are underground-dwelling faeries widespread in European mines. They are short and may appear seemingly out of thin air to make funny faces at people. So named because they make a knocking noise to communicate with human miners, knockers can be either a friend or a dangerous enemy depending on how respectfully they are treated. However, if they are befriended, knockers will lead miners to veins of valuable minerals as well as knock frantically to warn of an impending disaster.

If you should enter a mine in which knockers may dwell, doff your hat to them before entering and make sure to bring food and drink to offer. Never swear or whistle in a mine with knockers, as they hate the sounds of either. If you ever hear insistent and fast knocking, leave the mine and never return, or you may be buried alive or killed by poisonous gases.

Korreds, Kores, Korrs, Pyrenees—Earth

Celtic creatures with cloven feet, small bodies, and thin arms, korreds are hairy and have enormous heads. Their faces sport pointed features and even spiked hair. Korreds guard standing stones. Some stone circles and dolmens have been attributed to them as architects.

If standing stones have korreds in residence, they will try to scare away people who are not seeking the stones for spiritual reasons. Korreds will appear and make hooting noise to frighten people away. They may accept an offering of metal, since they enjoy its ability to conduct energy.

Korrigans, Corrigans—Water

Korrigans, meaning dwarves and sometimes encompassing faeries as well, come from ancient Celtic regions of France. Dwarves are always short and are usually not friendly to humans. Like elves, they can do all manner of evil deeds, from killing humans to stealing babies. At night, korrigans wear white woolen robes, and flowers in their light-colored hair. They look exactly like people, and are not too much shorter than a particularly short person. The only way you might be able to find out if a korrigan is impersonating a human is by asking him or her to name every day of the week, since they always leave out one or more, or try to change the subject to trick you.

By day, korrigans are ugly, and the men who fell in love with them at night usually reject them. Korrigan dwarves in particular love water, and will be attracted to play in fountains. In a myth that is perhaps related to the stories of sirens in ancient Greece, female korrigans can sing songs to make men fall in love with them. If korrigans live near you, it is best to give them a fountain or dolmen in which to play and then leave them alone. If you don't reject a korrigan for her ugly appearance during the daytime, she may be able to become human.

Leprechauns—Earth

Of course, leprechauns hail from Ireland, and they don't look like faeries at all. With dark, even gray skin and bright red noses, they wear red or green waistcoats and look elderly, even when young. Leprechauns are shoemakers for the faeries. Rather than wanting more gold to add to his hidden pot, a leprechaun would greatly prefer quality Irish whisky and tobacco for his pipe. You can find a leprechaun in an Irish tree hollow or in old ruined human structures like castles.

Leprechauns are moody folk, so they can be quite unpredictable. Beware a cheerful leprechaun, because in the next moment he could be drunk and irate, or even depressed and crying. Yes, they supposedly have that pot of gold under the rainbow, but they are quite wary of thieves. Leave a leprechaun an offering of pipe tobacco or a little libation of whisky to gain his friendship.

Another important tip about leprechauns is that you shouldn't spend all of your time searching for that mythological pot of gold at the end of the rainbow. They are actually quite the tricksters, and love to lead humans on a search for hoarded treasure that either doesn't exist or isn't worth the chase. The pot of gold is a metaphor for the good fortune that leprechauns can bestow on people. So don't plan on cashing in on some physical gold. Instead, enrich your life through forming alliances with people, even if they be as capricious as leprechauns, and you will find your own source of wealth.

Leshes, Lesidhe, Leshiyes, Vodyaniyes, Zuibotschniks—Air

Across Europe and India, leshes live in the woods and are rarely seen. They have the basic shape of humans, but they are made up of branches and leaves, so they can only be noticed when they move. Leshes are not very helpful to humans except that they attempt to preserve the environment in its natural state. Unfortunately for humans, that means that cruel pranks are played if humans in the forest are doing harm to the environment.

If you should see a leshe in the woods, you can safely leave it alone. They are solitary faeries and do not desire companionship. Make sure that you do not litter or destroy the forest you have entered in any way. If you hear noises that seem to guide you to the road or to other people, do not follow. Leshes can mimic any sound, and they often do so to make travelers lose their way.

Lutins, Follets—Air

French shapeshifters, lutins have no known default form, but they never take the form of humans. Lutins can be animals, mythical creatures, or even inanimate objects. When a lutin moves from one place to another, there is a flash of light as they seem to disappear and reappear. They are not terribly helpful, and can play pranks that are quite cruel. Lutins live in trees that are near water.

Most humans stumble across lutins when a prank is already in progress. A lutin will change himself or herself into a gold nugget or some other item of value temporarily, as a trick.

Look for flashes of light that tip you off. Also, a lutin can't hold a shape for long, so their pranks are never long-lived.

Mal-de-Mer—Water

French for "evil of the sea," the mal-de-mer have not been seen directly. The effects of the mal-de-mer are mysterious lights shining on the shores of Brittany and Cornwall that can lure sailors to wreck their ships on craggy and unsafe shorelines, thinking that there is a lighthouse or a city there. Caution should always be taken when at sea to navigate carefully around unknown land masses. Some sightings of the mal-de-mer lights have in later days been attributed to pirates.

Masseriol/Barabaos—Earth

These Italian faeries can live in either populated areas or rural locations. Those who love the city life are called barabaos, while those who love the country are masseriol. They are always male and appear elderly, fat, and red-faced. They are always well-dressed and have a startlingly loud laugh that sounds like a horse or a goat.

The masseriol are very friendly, and will help out with light housework, especially if asked by a female. They love women, and might be seen as harassing the lady of the house or beautiful daughters. They enjoy dancing and good conversation with lovely ladies.

Melsh Dicks and Acorn Ladies
or Churn Milk Pegs—Earth

There is a race of small English faeries in which the males are each called Melsh Dick and the females are each called Churn

Milk Peg or the Acorn Lady. All of them wear tiny versions of old peasant clothes and dine on milk, fruits, and nuts. In fact, Pegs and Dicks love nuts so much that they can cast a spell on nuts to give indigestion to humans who eat them. They are the perfect guardians for orchards, however, as they frighten away most thieves. You'll just need to offer them their preferred nuts and milk to harvest your fruit. Don't fall asleep in your orchard because, as a prank, Pegs and Dicks will sneak up and pinch sleeping humans.

Menehunas—Earth

Polynesian small people dressed in native attire, menehunas are tricksters who guard a fantastic treasure. They are known for their ability to grant wishes if they are captured by a human. Menehunas live near waterfalls and will hide if called by humans, since they assume the people are after their treasures or magic.

Menehunas are not harmful if you don't try to trap them or steal from them. In fact, if you are lost in the island tropics, they may feel sorry for you. They have been known to give food and water to travelers and even to emerge to offer guidance to lost humans.

Mermaids/Blue Men/Fish Folk/Mermen/ Merpeople/Merrows/Water Dancers—Water

The term mermaid derives from the French word for sea, *mer*. They are well known in the Near East, Europe, China, and India. They have the upper body of a woman and the tail of a fish and are described as beautiful, with long flowing hair that they love to comb. Mermen are the male counterparts, but they are not as well known. All merfolk love to sing, and can fall in love with humans. In Finland, mermen are known to be wise as well as handsome. They can cure illness, lift curses, and brew potions. Mermaids are considered perilous, as they can lure with song, just like the sirens of Greek mythology. They are associated with floods, storms, shipwrecks, and drowning. But they can also bestow favors, such as riches and good fortune. The merrow of Ireland and Scotland wear a red cap, and are gentle and kind. If the cap is captured or hidden, their tail will transform into legs and they will live on land until they find it.

Nature Spirits—Earth and Air

Most faeries could be fit into the category of "nature spirits" if you consider that they all occur in nature and have a love of natural things. However, some creatures can be described as nature spirits by their essential quality of living in only one type of natural object. Below are a few examples of nature spirits.

Jack Frost: A living force behind freezing weather often depicted as a man covered with, or made of, ice crystals. He is thought to be the artist who makes beautiful patterns that look like ferns in the frost on windows. Jack Frost is also a trickster, pinching cheeks and noses and sealing doors closed.

Jack in the Green: While Jack Frost is a frightening imp, Jack in the Green is the green man who represents life. He is the joy of the ancient woods, but can be a prankster as well, especially to those who don't respect his wild places and animals.

Dryads: The personified life force within trees, their name coming from the Greek word for oak, *druas*. Since the oak was considered the ruler of the forest, dryads are the protectors of all trees. They could be considered to be a type of nymph.

Radande: These are Swedish faeries of the woods, one living in each tree, according to lore. They give the fruits of the tree freely only to those who respect them.

While creatures like dryads and devas can move from one tree to another, often choosing the largest or eldest, there's an essential spirit of nature that dwells within each individual plant until the end of its lifespan. The Greeks called this kind of spirit a *hamadryad*, and it was often depicted as a woman with a trunk and roots instead of legs to show how they were inextricably bound to one tree. The best way to communicate and get in touch with nature spirits is to just trust your own senses when in nature. Go ahead and hug a tree. Does the tree seem spooky and cold, or does it seem to lift your spirits with its own inner joy? Don't cut down an old, strong tree that seems to have earned its own hamadryad. If you kill the tree of such a nature spirit, the hamadryad dies too.

Nymphs—Earth and Water

Nymphs are Mediterranean faeries that are always female, and thus represent feminine beauty and sexuality. Legends say that the natural lovers of nymphs are fauns or satyrs. Of course, in myths and legends, human men were often seduced as well. Nymphs are usually depicted naked or wearing only floating, sheer veils over their bodies. They look mostly like extremely beautiful humans, although some, called nereids, take the form of mermaids. Like devas, nymphs have specific purposes and domains. Dryads may be classified as a type of nymph that only looks after trees and forests. Naiads are freshwater nymphs, oceanids and nereids are sea nymphs, while oreads are nymphs of the mountains. Even dryads are often found near a water source.

Naiads are very useful in areas that are prone to drought, because they make sure that natural pools, springs, and stream beds don't dry up. They cannot survive without their water source. So, even if a pond once existed in a place, there will be no naiads left if the pond no longer exists. When humans drain their water sources, naiads die. Oreads don't just make the mountains look pretty. They are also the followers of Aphrodite, and thus bring love, romance, and passion to high peaks and low valleys.

All nymphs are naturally shy and don't usually allow themselves to be seen. However, they are more likely to respond to a human male than a female.

Ogres—Air

There are ogres in mythology all over the world. Ogres are usually about the same size as a human, but covered with hair and various deformities of the face and limbs. Ogres are rarely friendly, and often will try to eat humans. Some ogres may possess magical powers that are harmful, such as the ability to turn people into stone. Ogres are usually solitary and keep to themselves in the wilderness or in caves, so if you should see one, your best move would be to run away.

Ottermaaner—Water

Originating in the Netherlands, ottermaaner are night creatures that dance under the full moon while wearing otter skins. They travel by generating a bubble of water that floats through the air. They always live near the water and avoid showing themselves to humans. They are benevolent creatures as long as you leave their wetlands in peace and do not destroy their environment.

To work with an ottermaaner, try planting a night-blooming garden near a body of water that has no fish. Fish eat ottermaaner, and they will avoid them fearfully. They love flowers very much. Do not pick the flowers yourself, as ottermaaner become angry at those who show any destruction toward their homes. Contact them at night during a full moon.

Peg Leg Jack, the Fachan—Air

There may be only one of this Scottish faerie. It is not only one leg that he has, but also one eye, arm, toe, and finger. He has many hairs and feathers all over his body. When seen, he carries a spiked club. He lives in the mountains and, when disturbed, can be quite vicious. Peg Leg Jack is an envious creature and not friendly to any living being, especially humans. He should be avoided if you ever see his ghastly visage.

Pixies—Earth and Air

Pixies hail from the southeast of England, acquiring the name around the time when Christianity was taking over. The unbaptized Pagan children, or "Picts," were called pixies. Pixies were at first characterized as diminutive red-headed people, about four feet high. Those people may simply have been human children in those days. As time passed, the descriptions of pixies in myth and lore became smaller and smaller. Eventually they looked a lot like the classic creatures of faerie tales, frolicking about in nature with short hair, pointy ears, cute little upturned noses, and raggedy green clothes with pointed hats. They may, however, also be hairy all over their bodies. Some myths and legends claim they turned into modern day ants. Heather pixies or moor pixies are a specific variant that live in Scotland as well as England. Appearing as golden orbs or small people with translucent wings, heather pixies love to spin flax.

Pixies are usually troublesome creatures, and not to be counted upon for hard work that needs to be done. They would rather be destroying or stealing food or crops, souring milk, or simply pinching people and causing general trouble. A metallic substance called "pixie dust" is used by pixies for either good magic or trouble-making. Pixies are notorious for leading people astray, or causing them to become lost or turned around in the forest.

If they do help people, they do so only at their own choosing, rarely if asked. When a pixie is given an article of clothing or thanked for help, he or she disappears. What you can do to attract pixies is to make sure that your home is swept to welcome them. In lieu of thanks or clothing gifts, an offering of water can be given to the pixies. The water offering should be placed near a candle or the hearth fire of a home. Pixies love horses, so if you have horses yourself, you may find the pixies more likely to come near. But be sure to lock your horse up at night so that the pixies don't make off with it! Evidence that pixies are around your home include seeing pixie dust, mushrooms, and ants.

Poltersprites, Cobalds, Heinzelmannchens, Hutchens, Kobaulds, Koboldes, Kolbalds—Earth

Poltersprites are short faerie people found in Germany and Scandinavia. They wear brown shorts and brown or red felt hats. They carry pipes but do not smoke them. They can be either friends or enemies depending upon whether they feel they are getting enough attention and respect. In nature, they live in hollow trees, and if seen you should leave an offering of food and milk and take care not to let one follow you home.

If a home becomes infested with a poltersprite or a group of them, they will demand your constant attention. If you ignore them or are rude to them, they may angrily throw objects and make a terrible racket. The best way to move them is by filling the rooms with smoky incense so that they become irritated and leave of their own accord.

Queens—Earth

In mythology around the world, faerie royalty is frequently mentioned. You may recall Queen Mab from Shakespearian reference. It is said that faeries are governed by monarchy, and that faerie kings exist as well, but certainly faerie queens receive more attention in mythology. Another example is Queen Aine, an Irish faerie queen of the summertime, fertility, relationships, gardens, and abundance. Another Irish faerie queen is Dana, who rules over wisdom, peace, insights, solutions, abundance, fertility, and power. A third Irish faerie queen, Oonagh, rules over the hair on your head as well as the concepts of monogamous marriage. Greeks and Romans were not without their faerie queens as well. Flora was a Greek and Roman queen of spring flowers and fertility. Here are a few more queens and their domains.

- *Queen Cordelia:* Flowers, gardens, spring and summer

- *Queen Maev:* Femininity, menstruation and menopause

- *Queen Nemetona:* Trees, gardens, prayer, meditation

- *The Snow Queen:* Cold, cruelty, power, energy

Faerie queens sometimes reach the cultural status of goddesses, receiving prayer and petitions that would not be offered to other faerie beings. Some faerie queens have even strayed into the deity archetype (one is listed below).

- *Epona:* Celtic queen of protection, healing, equestrians, and guidance.

To best work with the faerie queens, treat them as if they are goddesses in their own right, even if they have not earned the title in mythology and lore. Instead of trying to make friends with them, or to trick them, be certain to give them offerings. Lift up your voice to them in prayer if you would like to ask for their assistance with any matter. Know that they won't show up in droves to clean your house like other faeries, but they may grace you with magical solutions to your problems. You may find that your troubles simply disappear, or you may find that you have acquired the wisdom in your own mind to solve the issue. Either way, if you pray to a faerie queen for help, be sure to thank her when your issue is resolved, no matter how the roadblock may have been removed from your life.

Rat Boys, Fir Darrigs—Water

Nobody knows whether rat boys came from Ireland or Scotland first, but they seem to have infested many human homes. They are not rats, but these faeries are definitely hairy, with tails and long noses. They wear clothes from the middle ages that are torn and worn through, and may carry a short walking stick with a skull on the end to scare people. They can also be recognized by their terrible smell, since they feed on carrion and seafood.

They may come into human homes from their natural homes in wetland places to find a warm place to dry near the fire. They are not helpful and may be quite mean, so they should be evicted from the house as soon as possible.

Sirens, Havfrues, Loreleis, Mary Players, Meerweibers, Merewipers—Water

Sirens, from the seas around Europe and the Mediterranean, are always female. They appear as the most beautiful women when they emerge from the water, but may take on more of a mermaid form in water. Sirens are known for climbing to the top of rocky islands in the middle of the sea and singing beautiful and haunting songs. Sailors, driven mad by the sight and sound of them, will steer their ships straight into the rocks and wreck. The only way to avoid a siren's cruel trap is to restrain oneself from hearing or looking upon her.

Sprites—Earth and Air

Faerie or elf type sprites originate in European folklore, and may refer to several different types of creatures, including pixies and any or all other faeries and even elves. Elves are generally to be warned against, since they aren't necessarily the beautiful people seen in the movies and games of modern popular culture. Elves, though not winged creatures, are often depicted as people with pointed ears and diminutive in stature. Though the earliest Germanic accounts of human interactions with elves showed them as either friends or foes, elves gradually began to take on a more mischievous and downright malicious role in folklore. In general, solitary elves were good and elves that banded together were nasty.

Many annoyances, from hiccups to nightmares, were said to be caused by elves. Elves should not be counted upon to solve a problem, or they might turn the situation into a riddle that is impossible to solve. Elves have been blamed for stealing human babies and even kidnapping full-grown adults to take them away to a secret elf land. In numerous legends, the person would escape back to the human world after a very short time in the elf land, only to find that everyone he or she had known had aged because many human years had passed. Dark elves, or *huldrafolk* in Scandinavia, can lick people with their black tongues to cause deformities. The image of a pentagram, also called an "elf cross," can be worn or inscribed to protect against the effects of malicious, elvish sprites.

Another sprite that lacks physical description is the buttery sprite from England, which has never been seen. Infesting butteries, inns, and abbeys, buttery sprites cause mischief, to be sure, but only to people who deserve it. Buttery sprites steal food from and get even with people who lie and cheat. They are, of course, particularly given to stealing butter, which can be made as an offering by someone feeling guilty of hypocrisy.

The word "sprite" comes from the Latin word for spirit, *spiritus.* Sprites can refer to ghosts as well, which should never be neglected in any treatise on faeries. Ghosts are found across cultures and in both ancient history and modern times, and many attribute the phenomenon commonly associated with faeries to spirits of deceased ancestors instead. In Japan, creatures called *yosei,* meaning "bewitching spirit," can raise the dead. Ghosts can be pictured as skeletal, shadowy, white, translucent, or even as perfect images of the deceased. The notions that people have of ghosts can be as varied as individual people themselves. However, it can be helpful to work with one's ancestral sprites, since everything we do in life is made possible by our ancestors having given us life in the first place.

To gain the favor of ghostly sprites, you can create an altar with photographs of deceased relatives. Take care not to include any living people on your ancestral altar. If you have a picture of yourself hugging a person who later died, for example, cut yourself out of the picture. Offerings made on the altar can be glasses of water or food the person would have liked during life. Even if you never knew a deceased ancestor, such as a great-great-great-great grandmother from Brazil, you can offer her traditional Brazilian food from her era. Ghostly sprites dearly love to be remembered, so you can include them in your prayers or rituals by naming them specifically, and also offering your honor and respect to all those whose names have been lost or forgotten.

Water Mannikins, Klaboutermannikins—Water

Old ships used to have a figurehead on the front that was carved to be as lifelike as possible. Water mannikans are German faeries that have no corporeal bodies, so they will find a ship's figurehead in which to dwell. A ship that has a water mannikin residing within it will avoid rocks, winds, storms, and rampant disease. If a ship should sink with a water mannikin on board, the faerie will leave the figurehead to help guide the sailors' souls to the afterlife, so that they won't have to haunt the wreckage. Since few modern ships have figureheads, water mannikins are rarely spoken of these days.

Waterbirds, Boobries, Waterhorses—Water

This Scottish faerie creature is not humanoid, but looks like a bird. Waterbirds stand about a foot tall and have black feathers. They can swim as well as fly and are active at night. You can tell a mythological waterbird from some other water fowl by the unnaturally long beak that extends away from its body, three times its height. If you were to look closely at its feet, instead of webbed water fowl feet you'd see terrifying human hands that are deformed with long claws. It makes a sound like a bull when startled or distressed. A waterbird can shapeshift into a horse that runs atop the water.

Waterbirds eat fish in the wild, but can be harmful to passing boats that carry livestock. Sneaking aboard, a waterbird will make a call that sounds exactly like its prey to sneak close enough to seize it and take it under the water to drown. To prevent being raided by a waterbird, you can either offer beef or mutton, or simply stay on land where the boobrie cannot fly or tread.

Will-o'-the-Wisp, Bob-a-Longs, Candelas, Eclaireux, Faery Lights, Fire Faeries, Hobbedy's Lantern, Huckpoten, Hunky Punky, Irrbloss, Jenny Burnt-Tail, LImniads, Night Whisperers, Ruskaly, St. Elmo's Fire, Teine Sith—Fire

Formless, flickering, glowing lights moving low to the ground, will-o'-the-wisps are always seen in groups. If you were to approach them, they might flicker in and out of existence, leading you on a wild goose chase. They have been seen all over the world, and have never been examined closely enough to know if they are faeries in their own right or evidence of another sort of faerie already known. There are those who think that they are the wandering souls of dead humans who are being punished by not going entirely into the afterlife.

Will-o'-the-wisps are seen only at dusk, night, and dawn. Other than legends of unbaptized children being stolen away, they are harmless to adults and Christian children. Sighting their glowing lights may even be a sign of protection, though there is no way to get close enough to them to gain more specific help.

Wind Knots, Folletti, Grandinilli, Sumascazzi—Air

These Italian faeries are difficult to see with the naked eye because they are small, translucent, and move quickly. However, if one pauses enough to get a good look, one would be able to see that his or her feet are turned backwards! Wind Knots can be seen riding atop grasshoppers while playing faerie games.

Wind knots are generally harmless because they don't particularly dislike humans. However, they do control the weather for their own amusement, and their power is so great that it is rumored their storms have even triggered earthquakes and volcanic eruptions. Making friends with a wind knot is a good idea so that he or she doesn't forget about you the next time a storm blowing a house down sounds like fun.

Yakshinis and Yaksha—Earth

Female yakshinis and male yaksha exist in Buddhism, Jainism, and Hinduism. They tend to have exaggerated sex appeal, with the females carrying fantastically large breasts and having curvaceous hips. Males have exceedingly broad shoulders that taper to relatively narrow waists. In mythology, they are mostly benevolent and giving creatures, but in some lore, yakshinis may tempt men away to kill them.

As a result, caution should be used with yakshinis, although they can help women who are having fertility issues or who are having difficulty raising surviving children. Yakshinis can be given trees to make them happy. In fact, they have a special affinity for ashoka trees.

two

Communicating with Elementals to Understand and Improve Your Life

*S*arah hated taking tests. As an accomplished law student, she had always been an excellent learner. Yet somehow, as soon as she was placed in a silent room filled only with the sounds of scratching pencils and the relentless ticking of the clock, she felt vulnerable and stupid while anticipating final judgment by invisible and arbitrary authorities.

However, Sarah was prepared for her test anxiety—she had performed a ritual beforehand, focusing on sylphs as representations of the endurable power of her intellect. It was to these sylphs she turned her attention after running into a roadblock. A simple question comparing two cases made her heart pound loudly in her throat when she drew a blank on one of the *case names. Calmly setting down her pencil with one shaking hand, she turned her face to the east, the direction of the sylphs' domain. A bright window there drew her attention.*

The tips of trees outside the window danced in the wind. Closing her eyes, Sarah silently half recited and half created an invocation to the sylphs from her knowledge about them and the experience and memory of her previous ritual. "Mysterious sylphs of wind and sky," she thought, "bring clear answers to my head, quick, fly! Aid me as I honor you in kind, help me with a brilliant mind. So mote it be." Her eyes were softly focused on the window now. She could almost see the invisible sylphs in the spaces between the swaying leaves, their hair and wings outlined by green. The clouds seemed to roll and boil with their presence. And, just like that, the memory of the case that was on the tip of her tongue popped into her head. Sarah quickly sighed a "thank you" as relief washed over her, and she continued with the test.

Understanding Elementals to Incorporate Them Into Your Life

In many examples of spiritual rituals, elementals are lumped together with their elements in the words of the working, so it might be hard for the beginner to tell which one is which. Think of the elements as building blocks for a house, and of elementals as the creatures who both live inside the house and construct the building. If you try to boss the elementals around or ignore their existence completely, every house that you would try to build using their blocks might seem to mysteriously disintegrate as soon as you finished, since the elementals were using those blocks in the first place. However, if you work in collaboration with the elementals, you may find yourself able to build stronger and longer-lasting constructs, as well as even being able to mix and match element building blocks that would otherwise return to their own nature and separate.

As they are sentient beings, even though we can categorize them and make some assumptions, they must be addressed as if they have their own agendas, since, in fact, that is always the case. For that reason, many magical practitioners consider elementals dangerous, just as any other entity—be it human or wild raccoon—would be dangerous if you put one in a corner and tried to force it to do your bidding. Why are elementals such notorious tricksters and potentially dangerous? Well, elementals have egos and do not exist only to love and help people.

So even though you might feel silly treating a bowl of water or a candle as if it were a person, push past that embarrassment to both protect yourself and establish yourself as a more powerful magical practitioner. You have nothing to lose but your pride, and you have everything to gain. You can begin a lifelong working relationship with elementals, and perhaps even count them among your friends. As with every other friend, your relationship is not guaranteed and will need maintenance. Get used to making eye contact with eyes that you may not yet see, and get comfortable talking to the air, as well as the sea, flames, and dirt.

How Can Elementals Be Dangerous?

It is only fair that you are aware of and warned against any potential dangers of working with elementals. The characteristic of elementals that calls for the most caution is their ability to hold grudges and have bad attitudes when provoked. So, unlike some other problem with Mother Nature, such as an ant infestation or a case of the flu (both of which might run their course or fade with the seasons), elementals may choose to stick with a person or place for a lifetime. There are several ways that this might negatively affect your life. Elementals in each of the four categories can cause health issues in the various systems of a person's body.

If you offend an air elemental, for example, it is not just destructive windstorms and shortness of breath that you must avoid. You may see your creative writing or public speaking ability decline, or things may simply seem to break when you use them. If it is water elementals you have angered, you had better be very careful around large bodies of water, and you also may have terrible luck in love. Those who have dishonored earth elementals may seem adrift in life, finding no peace or stability, and unable to hold down a job or permanent residence. Fire elementals are the most obvious danger. I once worked in a building that had three fires in the workplace's opening week! Each was seemingly random in origin, resulting from electrical problems, motors overheating, and other chance events. I wouldn't be surprised if it was a fire elemental at work there.

Elementals in Astrology

The influence of elementals isn't limited to our planet. The use of elements to describe the makeup of human beings exists in both Western and Indian or Vedic astrology. In Western astrology, elements can be used to paint a broad picture of personality characteristics for each sun sign, which is what you see when you look up your horoscope in the newspaper. Indian astrology ascribes elements to each planet. The sun signs and planets are both examined when looking closely at an individual's personality through something called a natal chart, a snapshot of what the sky looked like at the time of the person's birth. Think of the sun signs as a stage, and the planets as players on the stage, acting out a person's life. If you happen to have your natal chart, you can see how the planets either balance out or exacerbate the effects of the signs they occupied on your birthday.

- *Earth signs* (Capricorn, Taurus, and Virgo) are a deep lot, but are concerned with tangible matters. They are drawn to seek comfort, beauty, and deep connections during their lifetimes.

- *Air signs* (Aquarius, Gemini, and Libra) are concerned with communication and ideas. They can become thoroughly enthralled with matters of the mind, sometimes neglecting the practical aspects of life.

- *Fire signs* (Aries, Leo, and Sagittarius) are hot-headed and quick to leap into action. They also like to draw attention to themselves.

- *Water signs* (Cancer, Pisces, and Scorpio) are highly social and emotional. They can be healers, comforters, matchmakers, and the type to begin a revolution of art and feeling.

- *Sun*—Fire in Indian astrology and ceremonial magic

- *Mercury*—Air and Earth in Indian astrology, Earth in Western astrology

- *Venus*—Air and Earth in Indian astrology, Air in Western astrology

- *Moon*—Water in Indian and Western astrology as well as ceremonial magic

- *Mars*—Fire and Water in Indian astrology, Fire in Western astrology

- *Jupiter*—Fire and Water in Indian astrology, Fire in Western astrology

- *Saturn*—Air and Earth in Indian astrology, Earth in Western astrology

- *Neptune*—Water in Western astrology

- *Pluto*—Water in Western astrology

Perhaps the greatest use for elemental associations in astrology is to assess the compatibility between two people, whether they be friends, family, or potential lovers. The simplest interpretation is that if two people's sun signs share an element, they will be compatible, and if their sun signs have opposing elements (in astrology, fire opposes air and earth opposes water), they will be incompatible. The idea is that sharing the same energy level, emotional outlook, and motivations will help them find common goals. Of course, things are more complicated than shared elements meaning love. For one thing, each person's natal chart may have planets that add balance or imbalance to the sun sign's element, making the sun sign's element not as pure as it seems. For another thing, many people find lasting and loving relationships with people who are not normally compatible per se, because their differences complement each other, or help round out their rough edges by teaching them a different way of life. Here are the pairings you can consider.

- *Earth/Earth*: When earth signs get together, they like to respect boundaries and keep things traditional. When goals are shared, especially material or financial, earth signs can form an unbreakable bond of commitment.

- *Air/Air*: There is unlikely to be a lull in the conversation between two air signs unless they are communicating without speaking. When two air signs are on the same wavelength, they complete each others' sentences and find contentment in being truly understood.

- *Fire/Fire*: Two fire signs may fall in love with each other fast and hard. Both are impulsive, which means that there isn't a lot of time spent beating around the bush, but it also means that they are each likely to take action and then ask for forgiveness later. Arguments can be explosive and passionate.

- *Water/Water*: Intuitive water signs can become in tune with each others' emotions. Water signs are also content to go with the flow, and drift through life clinging to each other, even if no firm goals are solidified in mind. Water signs respect the action of going with one's gut feelings.

- *Air/Fire*: These two signs find conflict between the heart and the head when it comes to plans versus action. The air sign is likely to push the fire sign to think more before acting, while the fire sign has little tolerance for the air sign's tendency for armchair speculation.

- *Earth/Water*: It is the classic partnership between an earth person who values financial or material stability and the artistic water person who thinks none of those things should matter if love is shared. Each will push the other to let down his or her guard and find value in new concepts.

- *Earth/Fire*: Earth and fire people both like to get results, although the earth people may strongly desire more ground rules and boundaries to keep things fruitful. Fire people may struggle against the stability that earth people hold so dear.

- *Fire/Water*: When fire and water people share the same goals, the water people can add a depth of purpose to what the fire folks are doing. However, fire people may find the water people too wishy-washy, and the water folks may sometimes find fire signs to be too cruel.

- *Air/Earth*: Air and earth signs can build great ideas together into solid manifestation. However, care must be taken that the air sign doesn't slack off and make the earth sign feel resentful. Also, the earth sign has to adhere to the original vision and take some risks.

- *Air/Water*: Logic versus emotion can lead to turmoil or to a great partnership, depending on the respect the people of these two signs have for one another. An air sign can find a way when the water sign thinks something is impossible. A water sign can soften any cold facts an air sign doesn't like.

Evoking the Elementals Within for Protection

As you've found, you are born with natural traits from all elementals, albeit sometimes in unequal proportions. Later in this chapter, you'll learn how to cast an elemental circle, which invites the elementals to travel from their realms in the universe to stand witness in a place and time for you. All four elemental archetypes exist within you at all times as your internal resources. One ritual that makes use of this fact is the Lesser Banishing Ritual of the Pentagram. Ceremonial magicians call upon elemental ideas during this ritual. It can be used to exorcise bad emotions or spiritual entities from a person, or to clear a space of negative vibes. My mom and I like to perform it in hotel rooms to get rid of the spooky feeling of being in a strange place filled with the energies of others. I'm presenting the quick series of ritual movements and words here in a format that brings the focus clearly to elementals and to the symbol of their union, the pentagram.

The Elemental Banishing
Ritual of the Pentagram

Stand facing east, toward the realms of air. The first gesture you will make is to draw a spiral with your right hand, symbolizing how those elemental realms that exist outside of you also exist within. The spiral will start at your forehead and move counterclockwise to end with your hands clasped in a prayer mudra as you speak the opening words to all of the elementals:

You are (touch forehead to start)

The kingdom (draw a circle
counter-clockwise to touch your heart)

The power (continue the circle
to touch your right shoulder)

And the glory (continue the spiral
to touch your left shoulder)

Forever (end with your hands together
in prayer at the center of your spiral)

So Mote It Be.

Still facing east, extend your right hand and draw a five-pointed star in front of you with your first two fingers and see it in your mind's eye floating in the air. A five-pointed star or pentagram represents all four elementals with the addition of your spirit and is a symbol of protection. Plunge both hands through the center of the pentagram and intone the word "air." When you intone a word, you should sing it out loudly and in a monotone, as if you were ringing a bell with your voice, allowing the vibrations to emanate from deep within your belly at your diaphragm, resonating through your chest and your throat.

Withdraw your nondominant hand and put a finger to your lips in a shushing gesture. Your dominant hand should still be pointed through the pentagram you drew. Turn toward the south, the realm of fire. Your extended hand will draw a fourth of a circle around you as you turn. Draw another five-pointed star in the south with your dominant hand and plunge both hands through its center. Intone the word "fire." Again, withdraw the non-dominant hand to shush and turn to the west to continue drawing the circle with your dominant hand.

Draw the five-pointed star again, this time intoning the word "water." Withdraw your nondominant hand to shush and turn to the north to draw the final protective pentagram. This time, as you put your hands through, you'll intone "earth." You'll need to withdraw your hand to shush and turn to complete the circle so that you are facing east once more.

Stand with your feet shoulder-width apart and with your arms straight out at your sides, so you are representing the pentagram's five-pointed star shape with your body. Say the following:

Before me, sylphs, behind me, undines.
On my right hand, salamanders. On my left hand,
gnomes. For about me stand the pentagrams,
and in the center I too am a star.

Finish the rite by performing the spiral gesture and repeating the spoken words exactly as in the beginning. Upon finishing the banishing ritual of the elementals, the space that you have cleared should feel peaceful. You should feel that you have a balanced and clear head, and any who participate in the ritual with you should feel in harmony. You can do the banishing ritual of the elementals as many times as you like and at any time of day, to rid yourself of anxieties or simply to honor the elementals within and become in tune with them. It can be helpful to become fully comfortable and familiar with the elementals and their correspondences through a rite such as this before you begin attempting to use them for specific purposes in more complex rituals. Performing the banishing ritual of the elementals can also be a good way to rid yourself of any fears that you have about the danger of working with elementals. Yes, they can be scary beings, but they exist within all of us. You can either ignore them out of fear or begin to find your own comfort zone working with them.

Using Elementals for a Purpose

As mentioned in the Introduction, one of the many good reasons for working with elementals is that they can help you achieve specific goals through magic. Bestowing personalities, characteristics, and abilities on an element fleshes out the archetype into a potential living friend. Rather than just transforming the idea of North into a compass point on your spiritual landscape or the notion of Earth into the metaphorical furniture in the room, these concepts can become people; people who can guide, give messages, and travel to places and times of need.

In each elemental's chapter we'll explore some specific meditations, exercises, and rituals that can be done for purposes such as love, wisdom, divination, new beginnings, endings, and more. However, sometimes the light and simple approach of being more mindful of an area of your life that needs positive attention can bring about positive results. After all, as anyone with a one-track mind knows, focusing on your dismal lack of employment can make failed interviews and bad job opportunities jump out at you all the more, becoming more and more noticeable as the over-focus on jobs and failure bring negativity to the forefront of your mind. Likewise, no matter how much a single mom wants to find love, if she focuses all of her energy on her kids instead of leaving room in her life for her own needs and for a companion, that imbalance will make those love energies seem perpetually out of reach.

Ideally, all four elements will be balanced within you, putting all the blessings of the universe that are divided among them within your reach. So, how do you balance the elements using elementals? It isn't as difficult as herding cats. By surrounding your life with things that correspond to the four elements, you can turn your awareness to them. When you feel an imbalance, it can be simple to draw more objects together that keep you focused on that area of life in need. For example, earth elementals like to play among the sparkles of shiny rocks, and air elementals enjoy dancing with wind chimes.

Honoring Elementals

Some people believe elementals are very distinct entities with personalities and desires. As a result, honoring and placating elementals before asking them to be a part of your rituals can encourage them to be more inclined to ensure your success. This is especially true since all elementals are often thought to be mischievous tricksters. Whatever you can do to earn the respect of elementals—especially by being respectful—will help you to avoid being on the wrong end of a joke.

Setting up an elemental altar or shrine, or simply decorating your home with elemental symbols, is one way to begin honoring elementals. In order to please them, consider representatives for the elementals that allow them to "play" in their element. For example, an especially glittery crystal can be a delightful playground for an earth elemental, while wind chimes or burning incense allows air elementals to find joy in the movement. Large or crackling flames in a fireplace honor fire elementals, while moving water like a fountain may bring special joy to water elementals.

Salutations

Traditionally, elementals have been honored in a ritual context with a salute that consists of an open hand, a knife used only for ritual purposes called an athame, or fingers held up instead of an athame. The salute is done facing a direction associated with the element: north for earth, south for fire, east for air, and west for water. While saluting each direction, visualize the element and things that are associated with it. The examples below are intended to flatter and please the elementals without provoking them, and can be done at any time on their own or together. More information on calling elementals to a ritual for any purpose is included later in this chapter.

Earth

Salute the north by kissing your dominant hand and holding your palm to the north. Remember the most beautiful natural scene that you have witnessed on earth, perhaps a forested mountain top, a desert at sunset, or a lush rainforest. Visualize this scene strongly in your mind's eye and say:

> *Hail gnomes, elementals of the earth, strong and*
> *silent keepers of the green domain of the Goddess.*
> *I send my greetings to you in your realms. I offer*
> *you my respect and mindfulness. Blessed be!*

Air

Salute the east by kissing your dominant hand and holding your palm to the east. In your mind's eye you call up the memory of an exhilarating wind or storm. Keep this memory firmly in mind as you say:

> *Hail sylphs, elementals of the air, rising each*
> *dawn to inspire all God's knowledge and insights.*
> *I send my greetings to you in your realms. I offer*
> *you my respect and mindfulness. Blessed be!*

Fire

Salute the south by kissing your dominant hand and holding your palm to the south. Visualize a fire that warmed your body and soul in the past, perhaps a campfire or a holiday hearth fire. Keep the image and feeling as you say:

> *Hail salamanders, elementals of fire, kindling the*
> *will of God in all passions and desires. I send my*
> *greetings to you in your realms. I offer you my*
> *respect and mindfulness. Blessed be!*

Water

Salute the west by kissing your dominant hand and holding your palm to the west. In your mind's eye, recall the most beautiful water scene you can remember, such as a quiet moment by a stream, or a snorkeling trip in a tropical pool. Keep the peaceful visualization going while you say:

> *Hail undines, elementals of water, boldly evoking*
> *the feelings of God within all people who dare. I send*
> *my greetings to you in your realms. I offer you my*
> *respect and mindfulness. Blessed be!*

Cautionary Rules of Thumb with Elementals

As mentioned before, it is widely believed that elementals are mischievous tricksters at best and untamable wild dangers at worst. As a result, particular rules have developed in Western magical systems that aim to prevent elemental energies from affecting you at times and in ways you do not want.

Be Polite

The first rule of thumb is to always give elementals the courtesy of freedom. There are differing schools of thought on whether an elemental should be commanded or asked for help or participation. Many magical traditions include the practice of ordering elementals around or even threatening them. Using an authoritative voice with elementals is not necessarily wrong, but for now consider using phrases that sound more like polite requests. Pretend that the elementals are newly met family members you are just getting to know. In time, you may easily be able to call out demands and the elementals will know that you respect and care about them. But if a newly introduced stranger barks out the same command, an elemental may be tempted to react like an unruly child.

Another practice that beginners should avoid is imprisoning elementals within any sort of fetter like a statue, stone, or piece of jewelry. Although some people keep elementals in a physical form for rituals, it is a tremendous responsibility, far greater than for any pet.

A good friend of mine was once involved in magical practices that led him to imprison elementals. He grew toward a more peaceful live-and-let-live spirituality with age, but he still kept his elemental fetters. At one point, he showed them to me. One was a glittering amethyst crystal, the other he claimed to actually be a part of a human jawbone. Both objects left me squirming uncomfortably; I felt what seemed like a powerful force of rage emanating from them. Even though the crystal was beautiful, I wanted nothing more than to leave its presence and beat a hasty retreat from my friend's home.

Keeping those elementals required great energy and attention, all provided by my friend. After my visit, the events that followed in his life were related to his affront to the earth elementals, I believe. He was unable to hold down his place of residence or his job. He ended up having severe issues with his friendships (yes, including the friendship he shared with me), and he ended up leaving his social circle and spiritual practice behind. I can only hope that he has released the elementals and moved on with his life. Holding any entity against its will can also have consequences if it were to break free and do mischief or take revenge on your home or upon a loved one. Again, allow elementals the courtesy of freedom.

Give Offerings

Of course, giving a gift to an honored guest is part of being polite. However, more than just being a courtesy to the elementals, giving them an offering helps them to do their work. Think of it as a physical law of exchange, in which what you put into the working is exactly what you get out of it. Putting time and thought into what you might offer to an elemental will help you receive greater blessings from that elemental in exchange. Traditional offerings have included food and drink, or symbolic representations of the elemental. You can always add herbs as an offering to any ritual to increase its power.

Although herbs are mostly assigned to the earth elemental realm, herbs contain the magic of all of the elements of nature. Air is represented by the fragrance of the herbs. Fire is within each plant's ability to affect the body, and the source of the fire energy comes from the sun that fueled its growth. Water is in the plant's juices, but even in dried herbs it remains present in the residual energy from the plant's growth and ability to nourish. Earth, of course, is represented by the herb's physical manifestation, in the roots, berries, nuts, stems, fruits, and all other parts you can see and touch.

Add Your Energy to the Work

It would be kind of neat to have amazing creatures on hand to do your bidding while you sit back and enjoy the labor of your minions. I will admit that as a teenager I had hopes that I would be able to send a swarm of salamanders to burn down the home of my enemy while I cackled and reveled at my accomplishment. Instead, I ended up with my own coffee table set on fire and was forced to face my own fears (as well as my parents' ire) at my irresponsibility with candles.

If you want a creature to do all the work for you, consider getting yourself a horse. Elementals are the very definition of wild, and they will not simply obey the command of anyone who asks. Not only will you need to gain their alliance, but you will have to add your own energy to the exercise by both raising elemental energy from within through actions like dance or chanting, and by working toward your goals in the everyday mundane sense of making things more likely to happen.

Cast a Circle

It is a good idea to always cast a circle before summoning elementals. A circle is a magical boundary created in order to keep positive energies in and, often, negative energies out. You will notice that in the elemental honoring example on page 83, the elementals were greeted where they were but not called to approach the practitioner or do anything. For making requests, a circle is warranted to let the positive aspects of elementals reach you harmlessly, while creating a barrier against elemental intentions you may not want. Note that you are still allowing the elementals their freedom, as the goal of the circle is not to trap elementals inside, but to be a healthy boundary for yourself.

Dismiss Elementals

If you do summon elementals into your presence, be sure to politely thank them and tell them that it is okay to return to their realms and business as usual after your ritual. Stories abound in magical communities of instances where dismissals were forgotten. For example, a forgotten water elemental may cause flooding in your home, and a fire elemental left without a dismissal may be the cause of several kitchen or electrical fires. If you forget a dismissal, or you feel you messed up and did it wrong somehow, go back and do the dismissal all over again, even if you are halfway through it or if you have moved on to something else. More about dismissals will be included later in ritual instructions.

Start with Earth

If you are feeling nervous about working directly with elementals, start with earth elementals. In many ceremonial magical traditions, the first path of study is of earth. The reason is that the earth is constant, and earth elementals are known for their stability and relatively temperate personality when compared to other elementals. Begin by building an earth altar and hailing the earth elementals daily, as described earlier. You can also meditate on the earth element, which we'll explore later. Only when you feel ready to reach out to all four elements should you start invoking them in a circle.

Seek Balance

People tend to gravitate toward their favorite elemental. I'll admit that I love fire. Fire is warm, shiny, exciting, and just dangerous enough to hold my interest. As for the other elements, air is invisible and ubiquitous enough to be boring, I'm a terrible gardener and find no joy in tilling the soil, and I can't even swim in water. If I followed my tendencies, all of my rituals might be heavy on the fire magic without properly honoring the other elementals. Cultivating an elemental imbalance in your ritual space or in yourself can be troublesome.

When I was younger, I took my fascination with fire to a magical extreme, and nearly all of my rituals had fire as their focus. I would spend hours gazing into candle flames, trying to make the flame dance with my mind. Soon I was delighted to find some success in making the flame die down or pop back up again. I showed off to everyone who would come and watch me put out the candles and then grow the flame back again from the red smoldering wick.

My success made me focus more on fire elementals. Pretty soon, I found myself less able to control the elemental I thought I had made to do my bidding. Instead of lighting a candle, some papers on my table would catch fire. Or candles would light while I was sleeping, which of course is very dangerous. I started developing some blisters almost like burns on my palms. It happens that during a centering meditation, the palms should be the fire and water energy vortices, but it became obvious that I was tremendously out of balance. I became scared about my lack of control over the situation. I ended up solving the problem by learning to properly ground energy, and by never again going to such ridiculous lengths to perfect those silly fire tricks.

Your magic can become less effective without equal parts of all the universal elemental building blocks. You may also begin to overwhelm yourself with an elemental's nature so that you start to have trouble with that element in your ritual space or your body, such as burst pipes from water elementals or accidental fires from the salamanders. Try to include other elementals in your ritual, at least in the circle casting, which will be discussed further below. If you love to do ritual work, try to alternate the elemental focus of each ritual you do.

Bless with Representatives of the Elementals

Blessing an object, space, or person can be done by introducing the thing to be blessed to symbolic representations of the elementals. The most common example is to burn incense, which represents both fire and air, and to sprinkle holy water, which is salted water to represent both earth and water. Any object can become a magical charm by simply sprinkling and censing it, and any person or place can receive the blessings of the elementals in the same way. By bringing the elementals to meet your person, place, or thing, you draw their attention and show them that you desire their presence and good will. Even if asking for the blessings of a deity or some other entity, it is best to also sprinkle and cense to acknowledge the elementals.

Elementals in a Ritual Context

Elementals are used, at least indirectly, in nearly every Western magical tradition, especially when casting a circle. The reason for the use of elementals in any circle is because the four elements together represent all the ingredients of the universe. When a circle is cast, it functions as another world between the worlds. As a microcosm, any circle casting should include all four elementals. The number four itself represents a stable foundation in numerology. Stability is needed before you can achieve any sort of growth, transformation, or magic.

Seeing Elementals

Through the process of meditation or ritual invocation, many will be able to see visions of elementals either in the context of the magic circle or in the mind's eye. Others may not naturally be visual people, or may have a hard time catching sight of particular elementals. More about connecting with the separate elementals is in the following chapters. You can try scrying, the practice of gazing into a ritual tool to see magical sights. To see air elementals, try scrying in incense smoke. For fire elementals, gaze into a bed of hot coals or the flame of a candle. For earth elementals, scry in a bowl of very dark earth. For water elementals, a dark bowl filled with water will do the trick. See the chapter on undines for more detailed instructions on how to scry.

General Elemental Circle Casting

Step 1: Clearing the space

Before rituals, the space that is to be made sacred should be physically and energetically clean. Some choose to take a bath before the ritual. Sweeping the circle counterclockwise with a broom used only for ritual purposes can help cleanse the space energetically. Visualize any negativity or energies that are out of place being swept harmlessly away to dissipate into the earth.

Step 2: Grounding and centering

Now that you've cleansed your body and your space, your mind and your inner energies may need to be relaxed and centered so that you can properly concentrate. If you need a reminder about technique, see the instructions under the meditation for inspiration earlier in the next chapter.

Step 3: Establishing a boundary

With your dominant hand, trace the outline of a circle clockwise in your ritual space, beginning and ending in the north. Allow yourself enough space to sit or stand with any ritual supplies, casting the circle all the way to the boundaries of a room if you like. Keep the circle small enough so that any other people in your home or outdoor refuge won't accidentally trespass in it during your rite. Walk the perimeter of your circle three times while casting it, visualizing the line drawn in whatever way it comes to you. Some people imagine a white light, others a purple flame, while still others might see a bubble or tent with the mind's eye.

Step 4: Blessing representatives for the elementals

Each element should be represented by at least one object within your circle. For this beginner's circle casting, I recommend a bowl of salt for earth in the north, incense for air in the east, a red candle for fire in the south, and a bowl of water in the west. When these classic objects are blessed, the salt is added to the water to combine the two elements, and the incense when lit is a combination of air and fire, so that these two combinations are then walked around to bless the circle. If you decide to use other things to represent the elements, consider how you might combine them.

Again, start at the bowl of salt. With your finger, touch the salt and say:

I bless this salt to the gnomes,
as creatures of earth, for use in this circle.

Light the incense and wave your hand over it saying:

I bless this incense to the sylphs,
as creatures of air, for use in this circle.

Walk around the circle clockwise with the incense. Light the candle, saying:

I bless this candle to the salamanders,
as creatures of fire, for use in this circle.

Add three pinches of salt to the water, saying:

I bless this water to the undines,
as creatures of water, for use in this circle.

Walk the circle clockwise while sprinkling the water with your hand.

Step 5: Invocation

The circle having been cast, it is now safe to invoke the elements. During the invocations described below, remember to visualize each element. This visualization is the beginning of familiarizing yourself with elementals, and perhaps being inspired in the moment with new associations and revelations in your life that are connected with an elemental's domain.

Again, start in the north, and greet the elementals, saying, "Hail and welcome gnomes of the north, elementals of the

earth, I invoke and summon you to join and witness this rite!"
Raise the bowl of salt in the air with both hands.

Move to the east and repeat the salute with the incense:

> *Hail and welcome sylphs of the east,*
> *elementals of air, I invoke and summon*
> *you to join and witness this rite.*

In the south, salute with the candle and say:

> *Hail and welcome salamanders of the south,*
> *elementals of fire, I invoke and summon*
> *you to join and witness this rite.*

Finally, in the west, salute with the bowl of water and say:

> *Hail and welcome undines of the west,*
> *elementals of water, I invoke and summon*
> *you to join and witness this rite.*

Step 6: Do your ritual, exercise, or meditation

After your circle is cast, it is a good time for other ritual work.
You can also choose simply to meditate. On any occasion, you
may wish to practice clearing your thoughts with quiet and
receptive meditation, which can be useful before any ritual
action. Try focusing on your breathing while seated in a comfortable position. Try to synchronize it to your heartbeat so
that for four beats you are breathing in, for four beats you are
holding, and for four beats you are breathing out. Notice your
breathing and heart rate slow and try to allow your mind to be
clear of trivial thoughts, releasing them to the universe as they

come. You may not be able to meditate this way long at first, but keep practicing. This technique will help you jump into the more specific elemental meditations.

Step 7: Dismissal or banishing

"Dismissing" or "banishing" the elements is the process of politely opening the metaphorical door of the circle for them and allowing them to depart at will. The connotations associated with the words "dismissal" and "banishing" may seem like you are ordering them to get out or waving them away as if they are unimportant, but this is not so. These terms have ceremonial origins, but of course you will be acting more as a polite person in a hallway opening a door for an honored guest.

No matter what circle casting you choose to do, you should dismiss the elementals the same way. So, if your invocation involved jumping up on a table and inviting them to party, your dismissal should include climbing back up on that table to politely announce that the party is over. The circle should also be unwound in the counterclockwise direction since it was cast clockwise. For the circle casting above, start in the north again and salute:

> *Thank you, gnomes of the north!*
> *Please return to your earthly realms and may*
> *there always be harmony between us.*

In the west, salute again:

> *Thank you, undines of the west!*
> *Please return to your watery realms and may*
> *there always be harmony between us.*

In the south:

> *Thank you, salamanders of the south!*
> *Please return to your fiery realms and may*
> *there always be harmony between us.*
> Don't forget to salute.

In the east:

> *Thank you, sylphs of the east!*
> *Please return to your airy realms and may*
> *there always be harmony between us.*
> Give a final salute.

Finish opening up your circle by either retracing your steps counterclockwise and drawing the border back up into your hand in your mind's eye or by cutting the boundary of the circle and letting it fall away or vanish. Ground yourself again after you are done, as you did in the beginning.

General Elemental Grounding and Centering for Beginners

Ideally, grounding should leave you feeling rested and energized, as its goal is to establish a neutral energy exchange with the earth. Begin by relaxing and visualizing the energy in your body, perhaps as smoke, water, or light. Allow any negative, stuck, or excess energy to flow through your feet down into the earth. If you feel you need more energy, draw it up from the earth and see it fill you up in your mind's eye. It will take practice and experience to find the balance that feels just right.

A centering meditation you can do is one based on the elementals within. After grounding, turn your attention to the palms of each hand and the soles of your feet. Those are the locations of energy vortices corresponding to each of the four elements. Your left foot is the energy vortex used by earth elementals, your right foot by air, right hand fire, and left hand water. Try standing up barefoot and bare-handed, spreading your feet to shoulder-width apart and your hands out to your sides, as if you were a five-pointed star with your head being the topmost point.

Begin by focusing on your left foot, the vortex that is used by earth elementals. What do you notice about your left foot when you close your eyes and turn your attention to that area of your body? Is it hot or cold? Do you feel a sensation that could be attributed to spiritual energy, such as a prickly or fuzzy pressure? Do you see a color in your mind's eye around your foot? Explore your left foot with all of your senses and intuition. Next, turn your attention to your right foot, that of air, for comparison. Do you notice a different color or feeling in your mind? Take your time so that you can establish your own perception of the air vortex as well as develop a comparison between the two vortices. Next, turn your attention to your right hand, that of fire, and then your left hand, that of water. By now, you should be able to perceive and compare the four elemental energy vortices.

The fifth energy vortex is located at your head, representing spirit. There are actually several energy vortexes around your head, and different people feel that different locations represent spirit. Feel around for yourself and decide which location seems right for you. Some people use the one in the middle of the forehead, and some people use one that sits outside the head on top, like a crown, or hovers a little above the head. Energy from the divine or your higher self comes from within or from the sky to refresh the spirit vortex, so you may notice it looking or feeling more vibrant than the other vortices.

Now that you've found your most energized of the five vortices, compare all four of your elemental vortices to your spirit vortex. Is one or more elemental vortex less colorful, smaller, or feel weaker in some way? Allow energy to flow down from your spirit vortex to any or all of the elemental vortices that may seem lacking. You may see the energy flow in your mind's eye as a color, liquid, smoke, light, or some other fluid movement. Take your time until all five of the vortices are as intense in your perception as the spirit vortex. You will notice that the spirit vortex does not diminish in any way, since it is constantly replenished.

Through this centering meditation, you will balance the aspects and energies of the four elementals within yourself so that no single elemental holds greater influence over you than another. Centering yourself is vital before working with elementals so you won't have a conflict of interest when working with a specific elemental to better your life. For example, if your water vortex was out of control and working in overdrive, you might find it difficult to get a fire exercise to work for you, since your water energies would put the fire out.

You will note that I didn't prescribe any specific colors for you to visualize at each of the vortices. People are very individual when it comes to their energy, so I encourage you not to simply force yourself to see the color correspondences for each elemental in your mind's eye. It matters less what color a vortex might be than each vortex balancing the others. Allowing your mind to see your true perceptions will give you more valuable information than if you force yourself to conform to somebody else's vision of how their energy pattern looks or should look. After all, if you notice a color change happen in your vortices, you might be able to ask yourself why those changes are happening in your life and find an answer in your life choices, rather than simply forcing yourself not to see that information.

Take your time when first performing this centering meditation. You might want to record yourself speaking the steps of the meditation, giving pauses for visualization. After you've established a familiarity with your elemental vortices, the centering meditation will be more quickly achieved, and it will be nearly instantaneous when you are practiced and efficient.

three

Sylphs—
Elementals of Air

Think about how mysterious the concept of air must have been to ancient peoples. Nobody could see the air unless it was colored with smoke or ash, but people knew that wind moved the leaves of trees and pushed gently on their skin. What sort of mysterious force was brushing its hands through people's hair and shaking bushes day and night? Invisible beings, sylphs, were given dominion over the element of air.

Mythology

Sylphs are the essence of the element of air. Though, like air, sylphs traditionally can't be seen with the naked eye, they have nevertheless taken form in artistic renditions and in the descriptions of myths and legends. Sylphs have been visually interpreted as very small and winged. Perhaps you will find a vision, as well, of a sylph in your mind's eye, or find it in your imagination while on a flight of fancy. After all, imagination is the realm of the sylph.

Sylphs carry messages through the air, traveling so fast as to be instantaneous. They can also carry your intention to the concepts associated with air, such as intelligence, inspiration, and intuition. In fact, even the word "inspire" has the Latin meaning "to breathe air inward." When feeling a bit of writer's block or lack of inspiration, one may only need to focus on breathing deeply in and out to gain the aid of the sylphs. Sylphs can not only sharpen your psychic senses, but they can heighten your physical senses as well. The realm of music is also the domain of the sylph, since they are the beings that carry all sound through the air. Before making music or after enjoying a particularly delightful song, consider thanking the sylphs for their work.

Strangely, although sylphs make a cameo appearance in myths and legends, there is a dearth of lore about them compared to the more well-known elemental characters like gnomes. Perhaps the lack of visibility is a serious handicap for the visual human mind. However, in the same way that a beautiful score of music can inspire a painting, I encourage the visual learners amongst readers to be inspired to paint sylphs in the mind's eye.

Meditation for Inspiration

Meditating on the concept of sylphs can help boost your creativity and jump-start your imagination, since the element of air is the source of all inspiration and new beginnings. I like to turn to the concept of sylphs when I am experiencing a little bit of writer's block. To use sylphs in meditation, I encourage you to try an active meditation technique by creating a work of art. If you're a visual learner, as most people are, select tools for the visual arts such as canvas and paint or even simply paper and crayons. If you're an auditory learner like me, you may want to grab your favorite instrument and prepare to record a new song.

Find a place where you won't be disturbed, and surround yourself with an inspirational environment. I like to turn off my phone and go sit alone in nature. You might want to try finding a comfortable spot in your home, play instrumental music, and light some nice incense to inspire calmness and invite the element of air into the space. Close your eyes, and do some grounding and centering. Grounding and centering is a process to calm and balance yourself before meditation and ritual exercises. If grounding and centering are new to you, please take a look at the primer to grounding and centering in the previous chapter. You'll find that it is generalized to all elementals, not just sylphs, to allow you to use it in all contexts.

Allow yourself some time to become calm before you start your inspired artistic meditation, so that your heart rate can slow down and your mind can detach from the earthly anxieties of your day. Try focusing on your breathing. Breathe in through your nose and out through your mouth, taking deep belly breaths so that your belly button draws away from your spine as your diaphragm pulls in more fresh air. Try square breathing by breathing in for four counts, holding your breath for four counts, breathing out for four counts, and holding again for four counts before renewing the cycle. Square breathing can be challenging at first, but you'll find it gets easier the more calm you become and the deeper you sink into meditation, so don't quit right away if you are feeling like you are gasping for breath.

After square breathing becomes so simple it's automatic, you can begin to create your art. You can open your eyes if you wish to see your work as you make it, or keep your eyes closed and just make an abstract, freeform creation, which can be a solution if you find yourself overly critical of your own artwork. The idea is not to make the perfect representation of a sylph, but to put your inspiration in motion to live inside the moment of creativity. It is only in the pure joy of starting something new and making something out of nothing that you can truly meet a sylph.

When you are finished creating your work of art, sit and look at it for a while, allowing yourself to relax and meditate upon the representation of a sylph. When you feel relaxed but alert, you can end your meditation session. If you've created a visual image of a sylph, you would do well to place it in the eastern part of a room or other area where you need the inspiration of the sylphs. If you are too shy to display your artwork, you can burn it outdoors as an offering to the sylphs and scatter the ashes to the east.

Invocation for Purposes

The element of air is traditionally associated with the mind and the intellect. In contrast to the emotional aspect of your brain, the airy realm of the sylph has to do with words popping into your head, the beginnings of a conceptual form that you want to build, or the communication that needs to happen back and forth with an employer before you can land a new job. When deciding whether to use sylphs to carry out your magic, make sure that your need isn't something so emotionally charged with feelings of love or loss that it would be better suited to other elements. There should be a cool, calculating aspect to your need that makes it perfect for the sylphs to manifest swiftly and without fanfare.

Rituals for New Beginnings

Sylphs reside in the east, where the sun rises. The sylphs are the essence of a new beginning just starting to happen. Imagine sylphs as the warmth you can sense on the breeze that tells you spring is coming a few days before the calendar makes it true. Sylphs are the musing structures that dance in your head before you begin to build or sculpt something that will exist in the real world. Before anything we imagine can be created on this terrestrial plane of existence on which we walk about, it must first be created on the astral plane in our mind's eye. You can think of sylphs as the architects of the astral plane, doing all of the brainstorming and planning necessary before our wildest hopes can be made manifest.

Performing a ritual for a new beginning is a good way to help jump-start your intentions. A new beginning ritual is best performed during the waxing crescent phase of the moon on a Wednesday. Perform the ritual before you get started on a project, instead of after you have just begun. If you have already begun your project, you might do better boosting its progress by looking at the rituals for the other elementals.

As an example of a new beginnings ritual, I am going to show you a ritual for starting a new business. However, this ritual can be adapted for other new beginnings that you wish to celebrate or promote before they happen. Simply change the cast of characters invited to your ritual and the content of your inspired hopes, as they will be expressed as your intention. For this ritual, you'll need to gather together all of the people involved with starting your new business, whether it be two business partners or a whole group of people. You'll also need a piece of paper and a pen with yellow ink to represent the element of air and to call the sylphs' attention to your need. I also recommend you have a carbonated beverage to celebrate during the ritual.

Ritual to Start a New Business

Perform this ritual to collect and concentrate the hopeful energies you will generate. Cast a circle. Once you have cast your circle, decide, if you haven't already, on a title for each person in your new business. Then, present each person in turn to the east with his or her full name and title, to introduce him or her to the sylphs and ask for blessings for your new business. Here is an example of how that would be done.

Hail sylphs of the east, I introduce myself as Jane Doe, President and CEO of New Business Incorporated. I ask your blessings for myself and my new business venture.

Once each person has been suitably introduced to the sylphs, seat yourselves in a circle and draft together a formal business letter to the sylphs with the yellow pen on the piece of paper. Open up your carbonated beverages and brainstorm together as you celebrate. What do you want your business to look like in five years? Ten years? Or later, after all of you retire and have to pass on the torch to your trusted employees or kindred? Write down all of your wildest hopes as if they have already happened, and give a toast and thanks to the amazing things that are yet to come but have not even been started. When your letter to the sylphs is finished, each person should sign his or her full name.

Finally, fold your business letter to the sylphs into a paper airplane and let it fly in an easterly direction. You might all decide what the manner of the flight tells you about the potential success of your business. Does the paper airplane actually fly? That's good news! Does it veer to the right or to the left, showing that you will all need to be flexible as your needs change in the future? Or does the paper airplane make a quick nosedive to the ground, indicating that perhaps the sylphs do not yet support your venture and you need to repeat the ritual with some changes amended to your letter?

Hang the paper airplane in your new place of business, if appropriate. If not, or if you have decided on a different new beginnings ritual that makes discarding the airplane more fitting, you can burn it as an offering to the sylphs and then scatter the ashes to the east, out of doors.

Exercise Before Study

During my many years enjoying an excellent education experience, I was always a big proponent of prayer before study and exams. I was rewarded with a perfect grade-point average, even during graduate-level studies. It has become common knowledge that taking the conditions experienced during study, and recreating them for an exam, can help boost your memory. Repeating a prayer would be an easy way to do that before a test; much more helpful than overdosing on caffeine or wearing your pajamas as you did when you were cramming for the test.

An invocation of the sylphs before study and exams is an excellent way to pull the mental acuity that is the essential nature of the element of air and the sylphs into your own life in an instant. You can choose to close your eyes to allow inspired imagery to come to mind, or you can gaze out a window or look up during your prayer, as long as you don't look like you might be peeking at somebody else's paper during the test. Make sure that you take three deep breaths before your prayer, to relax and inhale the air that is the sylphs' domain. If you are studying in privacy, you might choose to face east when invoking the sylphs. Here is a sample invocation, but you can feel free to speak the words in your heart as they are inspired.

I whisper to invoke
the sylphs for whom knowledge is a dance:
Clear the mental air of ash and smoke;
of confusion and ignorance.
Let right understanding spring to mind,
with harm to none, and blessed be.
In return I give you thanks in kind;
my inspired hopes, so mote it be.

Exercises for Communication

Sylphs are the ideal entities to invoke when applying communication exercises of nearly any kind. Air is the space of instantaneous communication by telephone or Internet, as well as the space between two people who speak with their breath as their eyes meet across the air of a room. The element of air also applies to the thoughts and ideas contained even in slow-moving communication such as postal mail, which often travels through the air by plane.

A communication meditation using air may not be well suited to issues of great emotion, such as communicating with the dead or trying to better the communication in a love relationship, as those topics may be better suited to other elements. Rather, the airy and distant powers of the sylphs are best for communicating general messages, intellectual topics, data, networking, or swift business deals. Inspiration is the gift of the sylphs. It is not a good idea to force your will on another person to communicate with you, as that may bring an untimely end to your communications. However, sylphs can gently inspire other people with the idea to contact you, if they want. The example below can be altered to send inspiration to others to contact you, if you stay mindful of keeping free will intact.

Telephone Ritual to Get Somebody to
Call for a Job Interview or After a Job Interview

The most frustrating time when job hunting is when you are waiting endlessly for a call back after having submitted your application. It is maddening to have just gone through a successful job interview, feeling like you definitely got the job, only to wait for days or weeks afterward for them to call with their final decision. There are many communications involved that the sylphs can help ease and move more quickly. Sylphs can help with timing so your references are ready and available to talk about your wonderful qualities when your future employer calls, and sylphs can even help the words on your résumé jump out at your employers to cause them to think about picking up the phone. Of course, follow-up communication from you will also be necessary, but this ritual can also help you decide when an extra call will make you seem obnoxious and when it might actually make you seem like a motivated go-getter instead.

For this ritual, you will need either a dandelion puffball or a few bird feathers, ideally collected yourself from the outdoors. The dandelion puffball of seeds is preferable for starting a new job, since it symbolically plants the seeds for growth, but bird feathers are fine if you are not in the region or season for dandelions. You can use both if you desire. You will be setting up these objects as offerings to the sylphs, so choose a location for your ritual that has good air flow. Ideally, you'll be leaving the offerings near or within a line of sight to your phone or other communication device. If you just have a cell phone, you can leave it next to the charger by an open window, for example.

Cast your magic circle around the area in which you will be leaving your offerings to the sylphs. Face to the east to address the sylphs directly, and close your eyes for a moment to visualize yourself successfully working in the job you choose. Try to visualize the outcome, a happy and financially rewarding workplace, rather than the process of getting there, which involves your employer picking up your résumé and calling you. Focusing on the outcome instead of the process allows the sylphs the freedom to work their magic however they best see fit. Now, in order to raise energy and send the sylphs on their way, chant your hopes aloud. Here is a sample chant for this purpose.

Sylphs, take this offering with my aspirations
To find and keep stable employ
As these (seeds/feathers) are accepted, your inspirations
Will cause conversations of joy.
I send only good thoughts, with harm to none,
Free will freely wrought will be all that's done.
So mote it be.

Keep those light, floating offerings on an offering plate in a place with good air flow as close to your telephone as possible, at least within line of sight. By the time all of the offerings blow away, your employer should have called, if it was his or her will to do so. If you still haven't gotten a call by the time they are gone, it is a clear sign that you should call and make contact yourself. If the offerings don't move at all from their spot, despite having access to occasional breezes, it may be a negative sign for you. Something is blocking the sylphs' ability to assist communication, such as a reference of yours who isn't planning to say positive words at all, or a job that isn't the right fit for you. A refusal of your offering is a clear sign to start over from the beginning with a new job application, revised résumé, and fresh perspective.

Ritual to Conceive a Child

Of course family planning should always be undertaken with the guidance of a medical professional, and no ritual will replace quality medical care, especially if you are experiencing fertility issues. However, asking the sylphs for the best start in your family that a baby can have is one bit of complementary care that can be added to more ordinary measures.

In many cultures, it is believed that the soul of your future child already exists and is merely floating around, waiting to choose his or her parents. The intent of this ritual is to use the sylphs to carry a message to your future child's soul, inviting him or her to join you here on earth. This ritual can also be used by adoptive parents to send out wishes for the child you hope will come into your lives through the adoption or fostering process.

You will need a small amount of bubble solution with a wand, the kind you can purchase in any toy store. A ritual for fertility and conception is best performed on a full moon, preferably if it falls on a Monday. But don't perform this ritual after the full moon has reached her peak. Instead, wait until the next full moon if necessary, to gain all of the fertility benefits the full moon has to offer.

If applicable, your partner should participate in the ritual. Since this conception ritual has to do with the potential of the child you wish to raise to adulthood, only those who plan to lend a hand in the raising of the child should participate. If you're a single mother planning to use artificial insemination, it is not necessary to have the donor attend the ritual. Likewise, gay or lesbian couples should both arrange to be present, and if your relationship includes more than one partner who will be parenting, all parties should be present.

Cast your magic circle outdoors, or at least in a room with a window that opens to the east. Brainstorm together about what sort of adult you would like to raise from infancy in your life. Think about all the qualities and characteristics you might want him or her to have. Should your future son or daughter be a confident adult? Humble? Compassionate? Articulate? You might want to get out a sheet of paper and write down words together, circling each word and connecting it with related concepts to make a bubble sheet outline of the person you hope to inspire your child to be.

Once your list is as complete as you can manage, the parents should approach the east and use the bubble solution to blow those wishes out to the sky for the sylphs to carry. Take turns whispering each word into the bubble wand, and then blowing a bubble or more to encapsulate that hope for your child and let it drift out into the air. When you are done, thank the sylphs for bringing your baby to you. Take down your magic circle. If you are planning to make a baby the old fashioned way, attempt to conceive as soon as possible after the ritual is performed.

A Word About Weather Magic

Since sylphs are the essence of air, which has changing winds, temperatures, and pressures that govern weather, they have been traditionally associated with weather magic. However, weather magic can be very tricky, both ethically and in terms of reliable results. All elementals—especially airy ones—desire freedom, and they always return to their essential nature.

When attempting to perform weather magic, you are likely to have the sylphs simply ignore your working and have it fall flat. There is also the more worrisome chance that, feeling insulted, or inspired to emphasize their freedom to do what they wish, elementals may create some extremely dangerous weather conditions that are wild and uncontrollable. However, weather magic is a seductive form of magic, and it is unlikely that any practitioner will go his or her entire life without at least wishing that something could be done about the weather. So here I will offer some advice as to how to work safely with elementals if you feel that you simply must work weather magic.

Step 1: Consider the impact.

Weather magic can be far reaching, even if it doesn't backfire and create a natural disaster. For example, I was once in a coven in which one of the members wanted to work magic with the rest of us to make the spring more sunny and pleasant. While the weather had been a bit more dreary than was seasonally normal, we all politely declined to work weather magic on such a widespread scale for the area, as there may be animals, plants, and agricultural families who needed the ongoing rain.

If you want a specific weather outcome such as sunshine for a family picnic on the weekend, think of how you can get what you want without having to change the world for so many living things around you. If you want to have fun at the picnic and enjoy good food and conversation, consider asking for those outcomes rather than hoping that controlling the weather will give you the good time that you want. Similarly, if you want more rain to come, so as to not let your prize-winning pumpkins become destroyed in a drought, try asking instead for your pumpkin harvest to be abundant without placing too much control on how they become that way. As with any meditation, it is best to visualize your ideal outcome without becoming too attached to the means of attaining it, so that elementals that choose to help you are allowed the freedom to come up with imaginative ways of granting your wishes.

Step 2: When working weather magic, use the least restrictive means of requesting elemental help.

Many of our Western magical traditions contain the trappings of controlling magical methods. Ceremonial magicians have practiced this way of doing things down through the ages. Although these methods are not inherently wrong, they may not be advisable for the beginner when working with elementals on the weather. For example, casting a magic circle is used to concentrate energy, but it can also be used to attempt to forcefully contain entities like elementals. The use of a ritual knife to draw lines in the air adds a traditional flourish, but that same knife can also be used to threaten elementals.

Even if you don't intend to contain or coerce elementals, it is best to tailor your weather magic work in ways that show your good will. Think of it like shaking hands. The original purpose of the handshake was to allow the other person to observe that you did not hold a weapon. Of course, when you meet a new friend at work and shake hands, you're not actually checking to see if the person is holding a knife or a gun, and you are not showing that you are empty-handed. However, it is still considered a polite formality to shake hands, because it says "I am not hostile to you," and it would be rude to refuse the handshake, even if you don't normally wield a sword.

So, if you are considering affecting the weather, try to strip your request down to its core desire when speaking to the elementals. Don't cast a circle, and use as few tools as possible, and especially avoid any that can be perceived as controlling, such as a knife or a rope. You want to show yourself without any weapons in your hands as you come forward to the elementals as a friend.

Step 3: Make sure that you explicitly ask that no harm be done.

Many chants end with the words, "with harm to none" or "for the highest good of all" for a very good reason. If you're calling upon your higher self or a loving and protective deity, that consciousness is unlikely to trick you unless you have a lesson to learn. Elementals, though, are unpredictable, capricious, and sometimes downright malicious if they see a means to exercise their freedoms and their essential nature in ways you may not have envisioned. Think of them as young children testing your limits and boundaries, always looking for a loophole in your plans.

When I was a young child, I made up a chant that I used whenever I went outside and saw the sky threatening to sprinkle me with rain. "Hold and gather wind and weather" I would chant as I breathed in and out, running to catch my bus or jump into my parents' car in a parking lot. I liked it because it sounded neat when I chanted it and because I wanted the sylphs to hang on to their plans just a little bit longer while I got to where I was going. Well, imagine a toddler being told to wait, and you may have an idea about how I was making the sylphs feel. I asked them to gather wind and weather, and they did just that. They would usually hold it until a most inopportune moment, perhaps when I was crossing a street, and then unleash a torrential downpour. If I'd known better, I would have modified my chant a little, to acknowledge the will of the sylphs and to encourage them not to harm anyone with their weather changes. For example:

> *Hold and gather, if you please,*
> *wind and weather, harmlessly.*

Step 4: Invite and thank.

Most people are more likely to grant a favor if there is some reward involved, and elementals are no different. When asking for a big favor from the sylphs, don't forget to give them an offering of thanks at least. Giving a gift of food, drink, or things that blow in the wind are a wonderful reward for sylphs. Remember to invite them to join in with your work without forcing them.

For example, a traditional means of calling up the wind is to use a flute or pan pipe made from a horsetail plant. Sylphs are delighted by the air passing through the flute. It invites them to come forth and raise the winds. Think of it like setting up a playground for the sylphs and inviting them to play. You don't have to force a child to use slides and swings when they swarm all over them on their own. Likewise, your offering of music by blowing a horsetail flute can give similar freedoms to the sylphs, allowing them to collaborate with you on their own terms. Lovingly crafting a flute yourself out of horsetail can make it more effective, as can leaving the flute behind, when you are done using it, as an offering to the sylphs.

Hopefully some of these tips can help you to avoid the common pitfalls of weather magic. Remember that no matter how localized the changes, weather affects many people and living things. Try to be mindful not only of the feelings of the sylphs but of your neighbors if you feel you must attempt to alter the sunshine, wind, or precipitation in your area. Inviting elementals to improve your life while also not affecting the lives of others is still just as cool and powerful, and you won't have to feel guilty about unintended consequences.

four

Salamanders—
Elementals of Fire

In ancient history, the night was full of mystery and fear, and fire was the only way to dispel the darkness and keep warm. But why are salamanders, those small amphibians that live in damp conditions, associated with the magical element of fire? Salamanders aren't just mythological creatures, but very real little wet critters that scurry around wetlands and mud. It could be that, since salamanders often hide in the sort of rotting logs that are found in such wetlands, they may have been accidentally tossed as fuel for the fires in ancient times. When people saw little lizard-like creatures wiggling out of the roaring inferno and fleeing into the night, it must have been amazing. Were these salamanders created by the flames themselves? Did they have some mystical power that protected them from being burned? Where were they headed after having been born from the much-needed fire of the evening? The legend of salamanders began.

Mythology

The imagery of a salamander in mythology is based on the actual amphibians that walk the earth, so the variation in art and written descriptions is not as great as for some of the other elementals. In real life, salamanders are pretty amazing animals, having the ability to regenerate severed limbs as if by magic. However, many supernatural abilities have also been ascribed to the tiny beasts, such as an ability to ward off fire or even carry fire to burn down the homes of enemies. You can see a mythological representation of a salamander in any fire, even if real salamanders don't live anywhere near your region. If you gaze into an established fire, at the coals, you will see a flickering orange light glittering across the coals. That moving orange glow, writhing in the heat, is the essence of the element of fire, the salamanders of myth and legend.

Salamanders aren't just limited to campfires and candle flames in their influence, but also hold dominion over the molten lava that flows from volcanoes and the spark of lightning and other electrical energy. Think of the element of fire as being the heat and light that powers all processes, but that also holds the key to their destruction. Whatever salamanders have the power to harm, they also have at least as much power to help, so working with salamanders should always be done with caution and reverence.

Meditation for Energy

This is an excellent moving meditation to use when you need an extra boost of energy, such as performing in a sporting competition, or even if you're just dreading going to work or taking a long road trip to see some obnoxious relatives. Since fire is dynamic, and the essence of passion and excitement, this meditation will not put you to sleep, but is intended to invigorate the body and let you channel the energy from the idea of the element of fire through your soul and into your mind and environment. If you feel awkward about dancing around or allowing the spirit of fire to move you in a way that may not appear graceful, sequester yourself in a private place before beginning this meditation. Light a candle and some incense to invoke the element of fire into the space and to provide inspiration for the meditation.

Since this meditation is so high energy, I suggest grounding yourself both before and after the meditation. As you ground, stretch your muscles that need stretching, roll your head on your neck with control to work out the kinks, and begin to feel present in the moment by getting in tune with your body. A good relaxation technique is to work from your toes upward, focusing your attention on each part of your body in turn, stretching or tensing the muscles until you feel the heat of their movement, and then relaxing totally so that you can truly be at ease. Sometimes it is impossible for me to even notice I have been tensing my shoulders or back all day from stress until I give them attention in meditation, releasing the tension after a bit of stretching and flexing.

When you have gone through an inventory of your muscles, stand and relax while gazing at the flame of the candle and the movement of the smoke of your incense. Observe closely how the flame and smoke dance, and allow your body to begin to move to imitate or be inspired by the movements of the element of fire before you. Is the candle swaying softly, or jumping frenetically? Is the smoke smooth and flowing in one direction, or does it appears to almost tumble through the air? Don't try to copy the movements in a mirror, but let go and try to feel the movements inside your body. Move all parts of your body that are comfortable for you at your level of fitness. So if you only have flexible use of your hands, so be it. If you are more mobile, try not to get stuck moving just one part of your body, like your arms. Notice the movements at the base of the flame and try to copy them with your hips or feet, for example.

Ideally, during this meditation, you should be so focused on allowing your body to move in the same way as the element of fire that you should not have room in your brain to be thinking about what groceries need to be picked up that day or what assignments may be due soon in school or work. The element of fire is transitory and transformational in nature. Allow the movements to overtake you until you are no longer thinking about how they look, or anything else for that matter, and your body warms up from the heat of your exercise. Hopefully you'll even break a sweat and feel like the room is getting a little warm as well.

When you are suitably warmed up by your meditation, allow yourself a cool-down period by grounding yourself and stretching your muscles again. Do another inventory of your body, this time from your head down to your toes. Hopefully, you'll find that some of the muscles that were tensed as hard as a rock before your movement meditation will now feel relaxed but energized. At the very least, by practicing this meditation often, you should be able to command your muscles to relax more quickly, simply by staying in tune with your body instead of ignoring its complaints.

Invocation for Purposes

The element of fire is transformation in its true essence. Fire itself is a chemical process instead of a static thing in nature. A fire starts, consumes, and ends with a new result, different from the combination of things that initiated its existence in the first place. Fire is also ascribed to emotions that are similarly transient but transformative, such as aggression and passion in all of its forms, whether loving or hateful.

By its very nature, fire cannot be sustained. So if you are looking to use salamanders in your rituals, be aware that they will be your honored guests for a limited time only, and they will disappear as quickly as they appeared. Fire elementals are therefore best used as a catalyst in your life to get you started with something exciting, like an exercise program or a romantic getaway, rather than to sustain something long-term, such as a loving marriage or an assertive work persona.

Rituals to Initiate Transformation

Using fire in rituals is frequently done to release offerings to deities or other entities or to change a wish into something that will actually happen. For example, rituals could simply consist of writing something bad on a piece of paper and then burning it to transform that thing into something better. Other rituals could involve writing something good on a piece of paper and burning it to make it manifest in a person's life. From those two opposite results you can see that the essence of fire is transformation rather than outcome, so when working with fire in a ritual context it is important to keep in mind your true desires, rather than letting those fire elementals run wild in your life, turning everything into metaphorical ash.

Below is a simple ritual to invite transformation into your life. Since the changes that fire can initiate in your life are profound, make sure that you are serious about changing your life and have a clear idea of what you would like your life to look like after it has been changed. Transformation without a goal isn't a good idea when playing with fire, even if your life is undergoing an unpleasant transition already such as a divorce or a demotion at work. Delay your ritual until you have a sincere need to destroy what is old to create something new and a clear vision of how your new life should appear.

Cast a circle somewhere where you can safely kindle a fire. It is best to perform this ritual during a full moon, preferably on or near a Saturday to get the full moon's potent effects along with Saturday's power to create change, even if it must be in a destructive manner. Using scissors, trim a small lock of your own hair to burn. Before you cast it to the flames, hold the hair and think about any negative characteristics or situations in your life that you would like taken away and transformed. Burn the hair.

After the hair has been entirely consumed by the fire, go to the southern quarter of your circle and reintroduce yourself to the salamanders, telling them about your goals for renewal as if they have already happened. For example, if you have lost your job and are going back to school, introduce yourself with your full name and the name of a job that you hope to hold in the future once your schooling is completed. Hold a strong image in your mind of yourself inhabiting all those characteristics you desire and with your life situation completely transformed into what you wish it to be. Thank the salamanders and close your magic circle. Expect the transformation to be swift and possibly a bit jarring, since fire is not a gentle element.

Exercise to Confront a Friend, Lover, Boss, or Coworker

One of fire's characteristics is assertiveness, a tool many people need when having to confront somebody about an unpleasant topic. Please note that using fire to gain assertiveness is not a good idea for somebody who is already naturally aggressive. An angry and volatile person may need to turn instead to the sylphs to think clearly and with a cool head when communicating. Rather, this exercise for confrontation is intended for those who normally avoid confrontation at all costs for fear of bothering others or causing trouble.

Before you perform this exercise, think of the various positive fire characteristics that you will need when confronting somebody. For example, you may need assertiveness, confidence, and even a little charisma to help things go your way. For each characteristic that you will need, select a piece of jewelry; for example, a watch, bracelet, and ring. Ideally, you would use new jewelry that has never been used for any other purpose before, so it will be clear of all other energies, ready to be blessed for specific use in your ritual.

This exercise is best performed on a Tuesday during a waxing or full moon, the day before or the day of your confrontation. You will need your selection of jewelry and a red candle to represent the element of fire. Cast your circle somewhere where you can safely burn your candle, and light it. Facing south, ask the salamanders for their help. Holding each piece of jewelry one at a time, concentrate on the characteristic you will need during your confrontation. Trace the word for the characteristic with your finger on the piece of jewelry, and then pass it quickly through the flame of the candle. When all three pieces of jewelry have been blessed, put them on and thank the salamanders. After closing your circle, feel free to remove the jewelry and put it in a safe place.

On the morning of the day of your confrontation, take a shower or bath and then don each piece of jewelry as the first thing that you wear before putting on any other clothes. As you place each piece of jewelry, be mindful that you are also wearing each of those characteristics that you desired during your exercise. Go forth to have the difficult conversation that you need to have. Afterward, you can keep the jewelry in a special place so you can use it during future confrontations. Be sure to label the jewelry with the characteristics of your intent, or you might forget in the future. Take it from me, it is annoying to have a box full of magic charms and not remember what each individual one does, so you can't throw them away but you can't use them either!

Ritual to Get a Promotion at Work

Using fire to change your work situation can be tricky business, since fire destroys before it allows for something new to grow in its place. So, for example, if you were to wish very strongly for more time off from work, or for more opportunities to work from home with your family, the salamanders might just help you out by making sure you get fired. As a result, you must take caution to only use this ritual when you are planning to burn bridges, so to speak, as when transitioning to a newer and better role. There will be no turning back. As with all fire meditations, make sure you have a clear goal in mind before you perform this exercise, rather than letting the salamanders come up with their own idea of what your career life should look like. Otherwise, you could end up with nothing but scorched earth.

For this exercise, you will need an old article of clothing that you wear to work at your soon-to-be outdated position. Ideally, it will be representative of the position, such as a piece of a uniform or especially a hat, since a hat symbolizes a role. You will also need a brand-new article of clothing you can wear in your new position, such as a new hat, tie, or blouse. The new article of clothing should not have been worn before or used for any other purpose. This exercise is best performed on a Thursday, on or just before a full moon. Thursday has strong leadership magic, while the full moon will lend extra power.

Cast your circle where it will be safe to burn your old article of clothing, most likely outdoors. As with the ritual to create transformation that used a lock of your hair, first burn the article of clothing from your old job in its entirety. Keep in mind that you will be ridding yourself entirely of that old role. When the clothing has been consumed by the flames and the fire has died down, hold the new article of clothing and picture yourself in your new job role. Hold the vision clearly in your mind, and see yourself as happy and competent long after your promotion, instead of figuring out how you are going to get there. Put on the new article of clothing and go to the southern quarter of your magic circle. Introduce yourself using your name and your new job title, as if the promotion had already been given to you. Thank the salamanders for their help. You may now close your magic circle.

The exercise is done, so you need not wear the new article of clothing until you begin your new job, if you like, or you can wear it for encouragement during meetings with your boss or job interviews if you prefer. Since the article of clothing is magic, you shouldn't simply donate or throw it away when it is worn out. Keep it for future magic if you are trying to get a new position in the same role, or burn it when you are ready for another promotion.

Exercise to Put the Fire Back into a Relationship

Fire is the element for passion. Please note that while other elements may be more suitable for some relationship rituals, such as air for communication, water for new love, or earth for stability, fire is best suited for bringing the spark of chemistry if those other relationship blessings are already present. In fact, if your relationship lacks stability, this exercise is probably not the best one to perform. After all, remember that fire transforms. You may find yourself bringing in new obsessions to your relationship that, while exciting, might rattle the foundation of a blossoming romance. Instead, this exercise is ideal for a long-term relationship like a marriage that may have become a bit dull, despite the fact that plenty of love still remains. This exercise is best performed during a waxing or full moon on a Friday, to bring in romantic and sexual energies.

This exercise will demonstrate basic candle magic technique, so that those of you who wish to ask the salamanders for help with other magic can simply vary the ritual components. For example, in this exercise, you will need a red candle to represent passion, but if you were asking the salamanders to bring more fiery joy and sunshine into your life, you could use an orange candle, and if you were asking for more reverence and respect in your life, you could use a purple candle. These are just a few color correspondences that I find appropriate, but if you associate a color with a feeling, go with your personal choice rather than any list of correspondences. The tools of magic are simply aids to your own magical mind.

In addition to a large red candle, you will need means to carve letters onto your candle, so you can use a knife or a pen, if you don't mind ruining the pen's ability to write by getting wax gummed up in the tip as you press it into the candle. You will also need cinnamon oil. You can buy cinnamon essential oil, or you can make your own cinnamon oil by adding cinnamon sticks or powder to a bit of grapeseed oil and letting them soak for at least a month, from one full moon to the next. You'll also need a candle snuffer as a respectful way to put out the candle's flame; you don't want to blow it out and bring in the influence of the sylphs.

Your relationship partner needs to be in on the exercise, so don't perform it in secret. The last thing somebody you love needs is to be hit by the forceful power of salamanders without expecting it. The two of you together need to direct your positive energy into bringing the fire back into your relationship. Ideally, your partner will perform the exercise with you. However, if your partner supports your magic but is bored or made uncomfortable by the idea of directly participating in the ritual, you can prepare the candle by yourself with his or her blessing.

Cast your magic circle where it is safe to burn the candle. Before lighting your candle, turn to the south and ask the salamanders for their help. If both partners are participating in the ritual, you should both hold the candle while visualizing what you want your relationship to look like from now on. Then decide on one word that epitomizes the fiery element you want to invite into your bedroom: passion, spice, excitement, spontaneity, et cetera. One of you should carve the word into the candle. Afterward, anoint the candle with the cinnamon oil, starting from the middle of the candle and rubbing outward in a clockwise motion toward both ends, as if you were trying to unscrew the candle, into two pieces, from its center. After you have finished dressing the candle with oil, it has been properly prepared.

Light your candle to ignite the spark in your relationship, and then try to start a little romantic interaction as soon as possible afterward. If your partner is up for it, you can make love inside the magic circle, or you can close your magic circle and wait for the right time. Light the candle daily when you and your partner are home until it is entirely consumed.

Whenever you extinguish the candle, do so with a candle snuffer and silently thank the salamanders.

Ritual to Help Initiate an Exercise Program

Of course, you should talk with a health professional before starting any diet or exercise program. However, in my personal experience, the most difficult part about exercise is starting a routine you can stick with for a long time. The biggest mistake is not starting at all, but starting with too little motivation can either make your efforts fizzle out without even really trying or make you overdo your exercise right off the bat so that you never want to hit the gym again. Try this ritual to initiate personal transformation that can be sustained for the long haul.

Don't rely on magic to make the perfect exercise routine fall into your lap. Before performing your ritual, do the leg work to figure out what you think will work for you, and then perform the ritual to help motivate you to stick with it. For example, start out beforehand by carving out time in your morning to exercise, and make sure that you have the necessary equipment, gym membership, or knowledge to add a safe level of activity to your days. Then perform the ritual during a waxing or full moon on a Tuesday to add maximum fire and strength to your conviction.

This ritual is not just for weight loss, but can be used for any sort of physical health transformation made possible by a vigorous exercise routine. For this ritual, you will need a small food and drink offering for the salamanders. Be creative with your offering. If you are trying to lose weight, you might choose a very sugary food to offer to represent the calories you will burn. If diet isn't an issue for you, consider selecting a spicy or red food that can be associated with fire. For a drink, pick one with high alcohol content that will be easy to burn. If you are not old enough to have access to alcohol or don't wish to be around it, you can toss just a few drops of any liquid on a fire without putting it out.

Ground yourself, stretch out your muscles, and cast your magic circle where it is safe to burn your offerings to the salamanders, preferably outside and privately. Cast a very small offering of the food and drink onto the flames of a fire and turn your mind to the transformation you wish to make in your life and in your body. If you are working out for weight loss and tone, visualize your ideal body. If you are hoping for greater fitness and stamina, visualize yourself joyfully moving your body in a healthy way. When the salamanders have consumed your offering in the flames, you can begin to raise energy toward your goal.

If your exercise program is one you can begin practicing inside your magic circle, such as sit-ups, push-ups, or other basic workout routines, you can use these movements to both generate energy toward your ritual and also help remind yourself of your ritual whenever you begin exercising. If your chosen exercise program is impractical to perform inside your magic circle, you can also dance to raise energy, moving clockwise around the circle to stir it up toward your goal. Select a fiery chant you can use in your magic circle and under your breath while you exercise to motivate yourself. Since it will be repeated often, select one that is short and can be murmured as you breathe in and out during heavy exercise. For example:

Dancing flames, dynamic fire,
move my will and my desire.

When you feel the energy build to a peak, which may mean that you break out in a sweat and feel warm or sense a tension that can be released, relax and allow the energy of the salamanders to flow into you and through you. Ground yourself thoroughly after such an energy-intensive ritual, and allow yourself some time to relax and stretch your muscles so that you don't feel stiff and sore, which might sabotage your own efforts. After you close down your magic circle, take one more step toward your goal that very day, to get the ball rolling. For example, you can set your alarm an hour earlier to remind yourself to run in the morning, or you can email a friend to suggest that you become exercise buddies.

If you did not perform your ritual outdoors, take the ashes from the offering outdoors and scatter them to the south. Take a walk, or a jog if you're so inclined, and look for a gift from the salamanders to catch your eye. Perhaps you will spy a bright red leaf fallen from a tree or an igneous rock that sparkles and steals your attention. Whatever your eyes rest on is a gift you can accept from nature; pick it up and thank the salamanders for transforming the offering into a gift for you. Place the gift somewhere motivational, like an elemental altar where you can see it, or carry it with you daily to remind yourself to exercise. If every time you reach into your purse you run into a stone that the salamanders have given you, they may be reminding you of your inner fire and determination to become more fit.

Ritual for Protection

Salamanders are excellent protectors, because nobody wants the dangerous element of fire to be an enemy. After all, fire can harm just as much as it can warm and provide delicious cooked food. Some common protection visualizations include shielding oneself with a circle of fire in one's mind. Should you ever feel threatened, strongly picture a circle of flame leaping up high around you to keep enemies at bay, and the energetic shield created will ward away negativity.

For a more involved ritual, however, that requires another special offering to the salamanders, I suggest attempting to obtain a cauldron. It can also be used for any other ritual that requires a burnt sacrifice. You might associate a cauldron with a witch's brew, but it also makes a handy crucible in which to kindle a fire. A cauldron can symbolically represent a hearth, the center of your home and family, especially when a fireplace is not present. In times past, the hearth was not only the center of the family living space, heating the home and providing leaping flames for entertainment, but it also served as the focal point for cooking, making it the center of the kitchen as well.

One tradition is to gather nine different pieces of wood for a need-fire. The belief is that nine sacred pieces of wood from nine different types of tree will make a suitable offering to the salamanders when you have a need. Curiously enough, the selection of the nine sacred trees differ in various sources of lore. The different woody trees recommended are interchangeable, most likely due to varying plant distribution in different climate zones. So, rather than give you a list of obscure plants to hunt down, I'd like to suggest that you go for a walk and select your own familiar woody trees, the ones to which you feel drawn. The only inadvisable wood to burn is the elder tree, since it is sacred to the goddess of the witches, and out of respect it is never burned. You don't need a large log from each tree you end up choosing. A tiny stick will suffice, preferably collected from the base of the tree without cutting it.

If you do need to cut a small stick from a tree, find one that points downward, and tie a black ribbon around the tree branch, closer to the trunk of the tree than you intend to cut. Ask the tree for a gift of its wood, and then pause to allow any signs or feelings to come that will tell you whether to choose a different tree instead. Before cutting, knock on the branch three times to tell the spirit of the tree and/or wood nymphs or elementals that dwell there to scurry to the base of the tree and stay clear of the area of the cut. Some people choose to cut with a special white-handled knife or curved blade called a boline. It is used to cut wood for ritual use and never for mundane purposes.

Acquire the largest cauldron you can afford, as it will be useful for all manner of salamander rituals. Traditionally, the cauldron is made of iron, which wards off faeries. However, you can choose a cauldron of a different material if you wish, especially if you desire to work more with faeries. Select a material with a surface that is safe to be exposed to fire and water. The cauldron should be stable and raised on at least three legs, so that when you burn things you won't have to worry about the bottom heating up and damaging the surface underneath.

Cast your magic circle around anyone or anything that is to be protected. You can even cast a magic circle around an entire building or a large property. To perform the ritual for protection, you can either burn the sticks in the cauldron or you can offer them in token by placing them in the cauldron next to a burning black candle. If your need for protection is great, I suggest giving the salamanders the real offering, but if you want to perform the ritual many nights in a row, you can reuse the sticks by offering the candle instead. Dress the candle by anointing it with cinnamon oil for the salamanders, or a protective herb such as garlic, and by writing the word "protect" upon it. In the southern quarter of your circle, give your offering to the salamanders and chant while dancing in a clockwise direction around the circle to raise energy toward your protective goal. Below is an example chant for protection.

> *Salamanders of power's seat,*
> *Protect and ward with fire's heat!*
> *With harm to none but evil, spurned,*
> *Where no respect for flames is burned.*

If you are burning the nine sticks in their entirety, wait until they are consumed before closing the circle and scattering their ashes to the south with thanks. If you are burning a candle in token, you can close the circle and continue burning the candle, snuffing it respectfully with thanks if you intend to burn it several nights in succession. The cauldron can be kept on an elemental altar, in your kitchen, or near a fireplace if you have one. If you used a candle, you can burn a little of it each night that you are home, for ongoing protection, renewing the salamander energy with a new candle when it runs out. Or you can burn the candle or the sticks only when you feel threatened. Remember to never let a candle burn unattended, even if it is for protection. Salamanders, like all elementals, are tricksters, and they can play with candles in ways that you do not intend. You don't want to allow them to choose to protect your property by making sure that it is unobtainable by thieves since it has been turned to ash. Always be careful when you invite salamanders into your home. Thank them, and allow them to leave by snuffing candles and making sure that offering fires have died out, cooled, and their ashes have been scattered.

five

Undines—
Elementals of Water

Water has always been a vital part of all life, and even now is amazing and magical. Much of our cells' structures are made up of water, which we must continue to consume frequently to continue even basic functions. In ancient times, the necessity of water had to have been known. Its beauty was observed and recorded for posterity. The concept of water elementals may have been born from curious people watching choppy waves and wondering what creatures must have been magically moving the water from below. Even today, when you hear the sound of the spray of the ocean, or when a babbling brook carries lilting voices to your ears, you are hearing the chatting and songs of the undines.

Mythology

Undine is a Greek word meaning sea sprite. More than the other elementals, undines, also called ondines, take on the classic imagery of faeries. Though rarely pictured with wings, as they are light colored water-nymph-like beings, undines often grace mythology in the forms of beautiful women. Myths and legends seem to spill forth from undines into other stories of fantastical creatures. Like mermaids and sirens, undines are said to sing hauntingly beautiful songs that can attract wanderers. However, undines are not limited to the sea, but are found in any natural body of water such as a lake, river, stream, or even a natural pool of collected water.

The element of water is associated with strong emotions and life phases, such as love and death. As a result, undines are thought to be wraiths or ghosts in some cultures, lacking the sort of soul that a living creature might have. In many tragic legends, undines seek to marry a human man and to have a child with him to earn their own soul. Although undines have strong psychic power within them, their energies should be used in conjunction with the mental clarity of the sylphs. Otherwise, the strong emotions of the undines may cause you to come to the wrong conclusions when you have a flash of psychic intuition. Undines are moody, mysterious, and to be treated with respect—their capricious nature can lead them to curse as quickly as to bless.

Invocation for Purposes

Since so many people are drawn to working magic because they feel helpless about some topic they feel strongly about, undines may seem to be very useful creatures, indeed. Water is the element of emotions, which includes all of them, whether negative or positive. Water can be poured to wash away fear or anger and it can be imbibed to bring joy and happiness. Since water is associated with the west, the place where the sun sets, it is also the element of death and dying. If somebody in your life is sailing off into the sunset of death, water is in the tears that you cry. As much as it is the element of death, water is also the source of life and healing and can be a helpful element to honor, whether you are battling chronic disease or you are pregnant with new life.

Meditation for Divination

Water aids meditation, whether drinking it, sitting in a warm bath, or gazing into a reflecting pool. I highly recommend quiet contemplation in front of a natural body of water when you want to both relax and gain gentle insight into your feelings and the nature of your heart. Water is also the element of psychic power and understanding. So, for this meditation, I would like you to try scrying, which is a form of divination in which one gazes into something, in this case water, to search for imagery that can appear in the water or in your mind's eye.

For this meditation you'll need a black bowl filled with water. I also highly recommend a journal and writing implement. Sometimes, in the course of meditating until deep in a trance, I later forget what I have experienced during the meditation. It is similar to the experience of forgetting a dream upon waking. When water scrying, forgetfulness is especially common.

This meditation is best performed during a full moon, when psychic abilities are aided. Take yourself to some place where you will be completely undisturbed, since sometimes the mind can block the ability to scry when you are expecting to be interrupted at any minute. Of course, it would be best if you could meditate by a natural body of water, but it will work just as well with a black bowl of water in any home. Seat yourself comfortably, shoes and socks removed to aid grounding to the earth below you, and take some time to relax and allow distracting thoughts to float away from your mind.

Listen for your heartbeat. You can place your fingers on your wrist or neck to feel your pulse, if you like, and feel the waters of your blood pulsing through your system. Calm your breathing and allow it to slow down and become in sync with your heart rate, perhaps allowing four heartbeats to pass with each breath in or out. You should notice your heart rate slowing as you relax. When you can force yourself to think of nothing but your heart, you are of a clear mind that is ready to meditate upon the water.

Open your eyes and gaze into the black bowl of water. Soften the focus of your eyes, as if you were looking through the bowl of water, past it and deep into the floor or earth below. Keep steady breathing and focus on your heartbeat whenever you find yourself being distracted, and wait in quiet reflection for imagery to come. You may see pictures forming on the surface of the water or within it, or you may simply catch a glimpse of images in your mind's eye. You can close your eyes if you wish, or keep your eyes open if you are experiencing perceptions in the water. You might even be able to see the undines themselves. Allow the images to show you whatever message you need to see at this time. Don't be alarmed if you hear the melodious voices of the undines. You are not going crazy. When the mind relaxes into the alpha wave state of meditation, the same state that you experience before going to sleep and dreaming, as well as upon waking, it can be normal and natural to perceive voices.

After the images in the water have faded, unless you're feeling jittery from being ungrounded, try to write about what you saw before you get up or ground yourself. The fleeting images will flee from your memory quickly, even if they seem to be startling revelations that you think you would never forget. Writing them down not only preserves the content of messages you receive, but helps you to recall the actual memory of what you saw. Elementals can be mischievous creatures with riddle-like communiqués, so don't be frustrated if you can't seem to interpret what you saw. Your understanding may grow over time as you get to know your undine friends, or there may be some spiritual mysteries left for you to puzzle over for a lifetime. The same scrying technique detailed here may be used with the coals of a fire or a candle flame to connect with salamanders or with a crystal ball to connect with gnomes.

Ritual for Death and Grief

In Irish mythology, the land to which the dead travel is located across the sea in Tir na nÓg. In Greek and Roman mythology, the dead cross the river Styx. As a Wiccan, I believe in an afterlife called the Summerland, wherein my loved ones find rest and rejuvenation while they spend time as helpful ancestors before reincarnation. I visualize the Summerland across a large and rough ocean, even though it does not exist on this terrestrial plane. The commonality in such myths and legends is that the water cannot be crossed unaided. When I was grieving a significant death, I found that the choppy waters of my own emotions were impossible for me to navigate without help from a grief counselor. If you find yourself unable to move past a loss, please talk with your doctor for a referral to help you, so you won't find your own life adrift.

Since the death of my father has been the most difficult for me to process so far, I thought I'd share a brief story about him. It turns out that one night he proved himself to be an accidental magician, performing a water ritual to banish his sorrow regarding the year in which he was diagnosed with terminal cancer. On New Year's Eve, he wrote the year on a piece of toilet paper, tossed it into the toilet, and peed upon it triumphantly at midnight. I'm quite certain this action must have surprised the undines.

When he died, I know that we loved each other, but I still felt that there were so many more things I wanted to say to him. It was some time before I moved to a healthy stage of grief where I felt that I could communicate freely with him among my ancestors. The need to say goodbye is a common one, and I hope that the following ritual for grieving will help the bereaved find a sense of closure.

This ritual is a modified version of one in which I've participated, in which small boats holding candles are set adrift in a lake to carry love to the dead. However, I frown on the original ritual now because of the environmental and fire hazard that can be presented when flaming tinfoil boats are discarded into the wilderness. Instead, you will create a boat out of a piece of fruit, burn the candle within it, and then cast your fruit boat into a body of water.

For this ritual, you will need a small tealight candle of the color blue, an orange, a knife to carve a name, a bit of olive oil, perhaps a bit of perfume or cologne that reminds you of the deceased (or frankincense oil you have made or purchased), and a body of water. Even a bucket of water will do in a pinch, and fruit substitutions can be made, although I suggest an apple or pomegranate if you don't use an orange, since they are fruits associated with goddesses of life and death in various cultures and legends. If you use another sort of fruit, cut your fruit in half, eating one half and carving the other half of your piece of fruit into a boat that will hold a tealight. It is very difficult to make a hollow half of fruit that is actually seaworthy, so if that is important to you, I suggest bringing a bucket or cauldron of water into your circle to test. You can also make it temporarily seaworthy by making a larger boat out of tinfoil upon which your fruit boat may rest. Be careful not to litter at the end of your ritual.

If you use an orange, you can make the candle out of the orange peel. With the stem at the bottom of the boat, cut the orange in half, or leave a little more than half on the bottom so that the edges of your boat curl a little inward, making it more likely to float. Pull out the flesh of the orange. The stem of the orange inside the peel will be the wick of your candle. Simply pour a bit of olive oil, along with your candle dressing into the peel without entirely submerging the wick. Don't use too much olive oil or you may swamp your wick or sink your boat.

You can perform this entire ritual in a magic circle if you like, or simply prepare the fruit in it before the ritual casting of the fruit-candle-boat into natural water. Carve the name of the deceased on the candle and dress it with oil, perfume, or cologne by rubbing from the midline outward toward the ends in a clockwise manner.

When your fruit boat is carved, face west to address the undines and ask them to carry your message to the dead. Cup the boat and whisper your message into it like it was a waiting ear. Thank the undines and place your tealight into the boat, lighting it. At any point from this time on, you have completed the creation of the boat ritual tool, so you can close the magic circle or keep it up until you feel ready to take it down, remembering not to wander in and out of its boundaries.

You can allow the tealight to burn completely, and then cast the shell of the boat into a natural body of water. Or you can attempt to float the burning tealight in its boat, if you like. If you set your lit boat in a natural body of water, though, I advise you to make sure that any metal or plastic in the tealight is removed, and that you stand vigil until it burns out in a place where you could retrieve the candle if it threatened to start a fire.

A Healing Exercise

In mythology, the element of water is associated with youth, healing, and eternal life, from the fountain of youth to the Holy Grail. I find that the symbolism of water as a healing element is not only because water is needed to sustain life, but because water as a representation of emotions can show mind over matter. If you can control the rolling boil of your thoughts and attitude, you can heal yourself from within. This exercise is to bless water for drinking, asking the undines to enter the body to heal it with calm love. This exercise can be performed at a time of great need, and the blessed water can be taken to a loved one who is in the hospital, or it can be performed as part of your daily wellness maintenance, drinking the water to wash down medication or vitamins.

You will need some drinking water and freshly washed hands, since you will be touching the water with your fingers. You'll also need a cauldron or a bowl. I like to add a bit of lemon juice to my water for flavor and the healing properties of lemons, and also a bit of blue food coloring to honor the undines and remind myself what the water is for when I see it in the fridge, so that I don't inadvertently use it for other purposes.

Cast a magic circle during a full moon, preferably on a Tuesday, which has power to help heal physical illnesses and mend the body after surgery. Pour the drinking water into a bowl, add your extra flavorings and colorings if desired, and then seat yourself with your fingertips placed into the water. Visualize yourself completely healthy, taking care to keep a vision of yourself after healing is complete, rather than thinking about how you are going to get to that place in your life. Positive thinking and emotional control is vital when working with undines, so if you are feeling depressed and vulnerable, put off performing the exercise until you can handle your emotions.

As you hold your visualization, remember that your body already knows how to heal itself miraculously from a multitude of conditions. In each cell of your body are the waters of life and the blueprints for building your health. Turn yourself to the west and ask the undines for their help. Raise undine energy by chanting something like this:

Waters of my body, mind, and soul.
Undines combine to heal me whole.

Chant with force and joy until you feel the healing energy wring itself from your fingertips into the water, feeding it to the undines. Thank the undines for their aid and close the magic circle. You can put the water back into a bottle, or portion it out into several bottles if desired. Store it in the refrigerator for cool, healing refreshment during your time of need, and try to consume all of it by the next full moon, allowing the water to wash away all illness during the waning phase and to build up your wellness during the waxing phase.

Exercise for Gaining Control of One's Emotions

I've always had a hard time controlling my emotions, especially anger. I'd like to blame it on my culture or my gender, but it is probably a trait I've developed over a lifetime of poor decision-making when I felt rage coming on. This exercise is one that can be performed to quench a fire of anger the night before confronting a lover or coworker who has raised your ire. Hopefully it will allow you to avoid going to bed angry and will cause you to wake up with a clear head. This exercise can also be used to water down other negative emotions, such as sadness or fear. However, if you find your moods severely affecting your life and if they arrive often and for a sustained period, you should talk with your doctor. There may be an underlying serious illness affecting your emotions.

This exercise is best performed during a waning moon on a Saturday, to help take away negativity. You will need some water, a bowl or cauldron, some salt, and a wash cloth or aspergillum. An aspergillum is a bundle of herbs bound with string that can be used to fling water after being dipped. I recommend lavender for your aspergillum to help calm your moods, but you can substitute with other fresh herbs if you like, or just use a washcloth in a pinch.

Cast your magic circle, with the bowl or cauldron filled with water placed in the west. Ask the undines for their help controlling your emotions. Add three pinches of salt to the water and stir it with your finger clockwise. Adding salt helps to purify the water spiritually, in the same way that you wish to purify your heart, cleansing it of negativity. Once the salt has been added to the water in a ritual, it makes the water holy. Hold the bowl or cauldron and gaze into the water, allowing yourself to feel all of the emotions that you may have been trying to hold back. Visualize whatever made you feel bad, and don't hold back. You can yell at the water, you can cry into it, or you can simply study the emotions written on your face in your reflection.

As you charge the water with your energy, stir it with your hand or with your aspergillum, first clockwise until the water is spinning in a miniature whirlpool. Then stir counterclockwise, letting your force of will push against the flow of the water and change its direction, symbolically exerting control over the waters of your own emotions.

When you feel exhausted or you sense your strong emotions subsiding, relax and set down the vessel of water. Know that the undines have taken all of your negativity and allowed it to be cleansed and purified. You don't want to completely rid yourself of emotion, but you do want to be able to direct it in a constructive manner. Take up the aspergillum and dip it in the purified water, sprinkling and splashing it on your face, over your head, and on your entire body. If you have no aspergillum, you can give yourself a sponge bath with your washcloth. You can even upend the vessel of water over your head if it makes you feel better. Never underestimate the power of a cold shower to wake you up to a new reality. By the power of the undines, your emotions have been cleansed and purified so that you can transform them into constructive rest or action.

Drawing Love

The undines have always had the power to draw love and fascination because they embody the uncontrollable force of love itself. This meditation is intended to draw love to you as if you were a hypnotic undine. A quick word about love magic and elementals: It is important to always allow an elemental, as well as the target of your meditation, to keep his or her free will, to avoid the mischievous elementals from forcing the exercise to backfire on you. Tricky elementals love freedom most of all, and they always flee back to their essential nature, ensuring freedom for the subject of your meditation.

What sort of problems am I asking for you to avoid? Never name or visualize a specific lover when performing this love-drawing meditation, unless you have that lover's complete consent. Otherwise, you will be doing a ritual without his or her consent, against his or her will, and invoking the anger of the freedom-loving elementals. Trickster elementals might allow your intentions to become literally true while creating a nightmare scenario for you. For example, your lover might decide that you are like a beloved brother or sister. Your lover might briefly love you and then hate you, or might love you as well as another for whom he or she has greater affection. The elementals have endless imagination and energy, so don't put yourself in the path of their mischief.

Instead, when working with elementals without the consent of other people, always make yourself the willing subject of your magic. I acknowledge that it can be hard when you have a crush on a special someone. So, if that is the case, before your meditation write down a list of the positive traits that your crush has, like kindness and a sense of humor. Then write down what traits you must have to display to attract a lover with those characteristics. For example, to draw kindness and humor, you'll need gratitude and joy. If you don't have a special someone in mind, you can simply list your positive traits that you'll need a potential lover to see and enjoy before being drawn to start a relationship with you.

For this meditation, you'll need the list of characteristics you'll need to draw a lover and you'll need to pick a song that you can hum or sing inconspicuously. I won't give you a suggested hymn to the undines here, because that might be strange to sing in a nightclub or to hum when out among friends when you want your results to take effect with increased power. Your song can be a popular tune or a nursery rhyme that helps you remember good things about yourself.

For your love-drawing meditation, you'll be singing in the shower. So, I suggest that you initially cast this meditation on a Friday during a waxing or full moon, but you can renew it any time you take a shower if you like. Your circle-casting skills may be put to the test if you'd like to cast a circle around your shower for extra potency, so remember that you can draw invisible lines with your mind that can go through walls. In fact, you can visualize the entire circle casting in your mind without using tools and have it still be effective for containing your energy.

Once in the shower, face west and ask the undines to bathe you with the characteristics you need to draw love into your life. Sing your enchanting song as loudly as you practically can and let the water from your shower wash every part of your body from head to toe. When you are done, don't forget to thank the undines and close any magic circle you may have cast.

Now that you've mindfully offered a song to the undines, you can use it as a secret cue to them when you want to put your love-drawing powers to work. Hum the tune to awaken the undines to heed your call during social situations or whenever you might feel ready to bring new love into your life. You'll find that those who are drawn to the characteristics you named will sit up and take notice of you. Since this is a gentle and not forceful meditation, take your time to enjoy the attention, and don't forget to do your part to establish friendships and relationships with the people whose eyes you catch.

Endings

Just as the undines hold sway over the loving emotions that overpower us when we first enter into a partnership, undines dwell in the deeper waters that make us rage and cry when relationships have to end. I've already provided you with a ritual to perform upon the death of somebody for whom you care, but this ritual is one that can help you when a relationship itself dies. This ritual can be especially helpful when a partnership or other relationship ends without a sense of closure, leaving you with a flood of emotions that seems to have no outlet.

This ritual enlists the help of the undines as well as the power of the written word, and variations upon it have been found in many cultures, including ancient Egypt. You will need a pen with black, water-soluble ink, a piece of porous paper like a coffee filter or napkin, and a bowl or cauldron of water. You may wish to also use a photograph or any other memento from your relationship to bring up emotions during your ritual.

Cast your magic circle and face west to ask the undines to help you bid farewell to your relationship. If you are having a mutual parting, it is perfectly fine to have your ex participate in the ritual with you, but this rite is designed to help you say goodbye if you are lacking that sort of closure. Write a farewell letter to your relationship on the piece of paper. Evoke as much emotion in yourself as you can, letting tears fall on the letter if possible, including any memories that you cherish as well as regrets that you may have. When you've communicated all that you have to say, immerse the paper in the water and stir it counterclockwise, allowing the ink to dissolve from the paper.

The idea behind this simple exercise is that written words are extremely powerful thoughtforms. As you create the words on paper, you give life to your memories and regrets on the astral plane. Once immersed in water, with the help of the undines, those strong emotions are dispersed to their rightful places in your life so that you can move on in a healthy way. Thank the undines for their help. To dispose of the materials, you can bury or dry out and burn the paper. Pour the water into a body of running water. Ideally, you would go to a natural river or stream to dispose of the water, but in a pinch you can use a sink with the faucet turned on.

Dreams

Water is the element of dreams and psychic visions. Before performing this ritual, which is designed to find answers and understanding from your dreams, you may need some preparation if you have never done spiritual work with dreams before. First, I recommend performing the scrying meditation discussed in this chapter to see how undines appear to you as well as to get the visual psychic part of your brain working. Second, and this part is considerably harder, I'd advise starting a dream journal at least several days in advance of your ritual.

Keeping a dream journal is one of the first pieces of advice that I give to anyone who wants to work with his or her own psychic power, but I admit it is very hard. You'll need the discipline and presence of mind to awaken fully after a dream, even in the middle of the night, turn on the light, and write it down in a physical journal before the memories begin to swim away from your mind. It is so much easier to roll over and go back to sleep. Rather than insulting the undines by ignoring a dream message they may send to you, I recommend starting the habit of keeping a regular dream journal before asking for their assistance. All elementals are very quick to feel insulted, and emotional undines are especially so. If you are unable to make yourself keep a dream journal, put this ritual off until you can.

This ritual is best performed if you want to find spiritual communication with the undines in your world of dreams, such as if you have questions about an emotional matter in life. You can also use this ritual to gain more control of your dreams if you are finding yourself prone to nightmares. If you think that you are unable to dream, or if you find your sleep disrupted or not restful, you may need to discuss this problem with your doctor before you throw undines into the mix.

To invite the undines into your dreams, you can quite simply have a relaxing bath before bed. Draw a bath and add a bit of salt and lavender to make the water holy, purifying, and relaxing. Light a few candles and dim the lighting in the bathroom. I also recommend a hot mug of chamomile tea to help relax and hydrate yourself during a long soak. If you want to try scrying in your bathwater, I recommend avoiding adding anything else like bubble bath solution.

You can visualize casting a circle around your bathtub without any tools, similar to the suggestion in the ritual centered around the shower. Sink into the tub as low as you can, so that your eyes are nearly level with the water. Ask the undines for their help understanding whatever issue it is that you wish to confront in your dreams. Think strongly about what sort of answers or insight you would like to receive, and what emotions you would like to feel after solving your problem.

Open your eyes and gaze with a soft focus across the top of the water in the bathtub. Allow your eyes to wander to any flickers of light you may see, such as reflections of the candlelight on the surface of the water. You may be able to scry and catch sight of the undines giving you a sign that they will come to your aid. Hold this state of quiet reflection as long as you can keep your mind from wandering and your body from becoming uncomfortable in the tub. Close your magic circle and extinguish the candles.

After your bath, go to bed as soon as you can. If you still feel up to it, you may want to cast a circle around your bed, though you should use representations other than incense or candles for the elements of air and fire, since you don't want to leave any of those burning while you are sleeping. It is recommended that you sleep alone unless you have a bedmate who is as committed as you to not break the circle until morning. Pets can move freely in and out of a magic circle. It might be a good idea to cast your circle so large so that it includes the closest bathroom.

When you awaken from a dream, even if it is in the middle of the night, be sure to write down all memory of the dream in your dream journal right away, even if it does not seem like a message from the undines. Dream messages may seem more clear when you read them later on, or you may find that the first dream only makes sense within the context of other dreams that you will have later in the night. Resume your sleep and record any dream that you have upon waking, rather than waiting until the morning. When morning arrives and all dreams have been dutifully logged, you may take down any magic circle if you chose to cast one. Remember to thank the undines for their help.

six

Gnomes—
Elementals of Earth

Ancient people may not have thought of the earth as a planet, but rather as our home and an ever-present force below our feet. How mysterious it must have been to see giant boulders in the forest and beautiful crystals peeking out from the matte surface of gray rocks. It must have been unimaginably terrifying to sense an earthquake shaking the foundation with a force that could only be attributed to the supernatural power of gnomes.

Mythology

Gnomes as elementals are not to be confused with the cheerful, imaginary characters of popular culture. Though it is true they love gardening, it is more because they love everything growing out of the earth, and assist its energies from underneath rather than kneeling down with gloves in the garden bed. We may have all seen depictions of garden gnomes with their pointy hats and big smiles, usually frolicking with plants and animals. Although short in stature like their cartoon counterparts (and often male and elderly looking regardless of age), elemental gnomes in mythology were not happy to be around human homes, preferring to live out of sight underground. Their eyes are small, and their noses are pointy and narrow.

Perhaps because the earth is where jewels are born, it has been thought that gnomes desire and fiercely guard gemstones and precious metals. Some believe that gnomes exist in every sparkle of every crystal, and that it is the magic of the elemental gnome that gives value to gold, silver, and gems. It is, indeed, a magical mystery that substances like gold have gained and retained value in every culture in the world throughout human history. Gnomes can help you understand the material value of things. While sylphs are the intellectual communicators of the elemental world, gnomes are the brooding scientists that seek to understand the nature of the molecules of the earth, and with it they perform their own magic and alchemy.

So focused are gnomes on the material that they may seem unfriendly to humans or uninterested at best. One reason for this may be that gnomes experience time and space in a different way than we do, which affords them the time and attention to monitor prolonged earth processes. A spiritual understanding of this is energetic "vibration." Creatures with a lower energetic vibration than humans may experience our years or lifetimes as short blips in their own minds. Incidentally, it is a higher vibration that allows sylphs to carry messages so quickly through the air in our perception.

Invocation for Purposes

Since earth is the element that represents all material, solid things, it might just be one of the most-used elementals in ritual work. After all, most people want to increase their cash supply or gain other wonderful things in their lives. Since the earth is also associated with stability, gnomes can also help with establishing anything that you want to have as a lasting foundation in your life. Though fire and water make frequent appearances in magical rituals, you'll find that there are many other props that fit into the category of the element of earth simply due to their solid manifestation on earth. Though undines are best suited for love rituals with high emotion, gnomes are helpful with friendships if you want to have, or already have, a best friend as a fixture in your life. This is in spite of the fact that the gnomes themselves are not particularly friendly to humans.

Gnome Meditation for Restful Sleep

Normally, it is the goal of meditation to resist the urge to go to sleep, and instead keep your brain processing at a relaxed level of function. However, this meditation is designed to promote healthy sleep, as well as to allow one to get in tune with the earth through its elemental. If you struggle with being able to get to sleep, practicing this meditation every night may be a key that you can use to unlock sleep for your own body. After getting used to the meditation, you may only need to start meditating in this way to fall asleep almost instantly. The essential nature of earth is its relative stillness and stability when compared with the other three elements. By allowing your body to come to rest in its own stillness, you connect with the earth elementals within.

Sometimes sleep feels hard to do because it feels like one is losing control as consciousness slips away during the normal early stages of sleep. Since this meditation is a sort of spirit journey down to the earth elementals, if you fear this loss of control and feeling of slipping away from your body, those feelings may be intensified during the meditation. If you wish, you can hold a rock in your dominant hand during the meditation for its magical powers of stability and grounding. If you decide that you don't like the feeling of falling asleep, and you want to return to your normal awake and energetic self, turn your attention to the rock you carry in your hand, and it will help to bring you back.

Begin your meditation in bed, of course. I like to lie on the floor or even in a grassy field to connect even more closely with the earth, but this certainly isn't necessary. Whisper to the gnomes, asking them to aid your sleep and to protect your body where it lies, the way they protect their most precious of treasures.

Close your eyes and turn your attention to your physical body where it connects with whatever surface is beneath you. Starting with the back of your head down to your neck and shoulders, relax and allow your muscles to feel heavy, so that it feels like you are melting downward. Become aware of gravity pulling you against your resting place. Continue moving your focus down your body toward your toes. Your entire body should feel like it is heavier than it normally is when you have completed relaxing all of your muscles.

Now it is time for your visualization to begin. In your mind's eye, imagine that you look around the room or area in which you lie and notice a hole in the ground that is the opening to the mouth of a large cave. You can jump into the cave entrance, or walk carefully down into it if you choose. As you enter the large chamber of the cave, stop and allow yourself to take notice of your surroundings. This cave represents your Mother Earth, so you should find it to be comforting. When I perform this meditation, the cave feels very warm to me and the rocks are quite beautiful and smooth. It is okay if your visualization differs.

As your eyes adjust to the darkness, ask the gnomes to allow you to proceed safely. Though gnomes don't normally like to approach humans, you may sense them backing away and allowing you to proceed forward even if you don't catch sight of them. Walk forward when you feel ready. As you proceed downward, let yourself travel into the reaches of the cave. These tunnels become smaller and begin to enclose you in the warm, dark womb of the earth. You may find yourself stooping down and perhaps even going down to your hands and knees to travel forward. Finally when the confines of the smooth rock around you are too small for you to continue your journey, let yourself rest comfortably in the darkness and quiet. Listen for the sounds of the gnomes working in the deep rock around you. You might hear your heartbeat reverberating from the walls that surround you, as if it were the beating heart of Mother Earth herself.

This meditation should allow you to drift off to a sleep that is safe and healthy. When you wake up, you should feel refreshed, and may have a memory of dreams exploring the realms of the gnomes underground. If you decide to end your meditation early, before you fall asleep, turn your attention to the rock you hold in your hand, and you should feel yourself swiftly withdrawing back into the waking world without having to retrace your steps groggily through the cave. Since this meditation is so relaxing, you may wish to rest before getting up on your feet, and make sure you feel grounded before moving again.

Ritual for Home Blessing

People worry about moving into a house that is haunted or built upon an ancient sacred burial place. Well, every home is built upon sacred ground, accurately enough. As the gnomes are elementals of earth, they exist in every place on the earth. When we build homes or places to work and live, we don't displace the gnomes. Instead, we work alongside them. To have a happier, more stable home, we would do well to ask for the blessings of the gnomes that lived there first.

As has been mentioned before, gnomes do not like to be best buddies with people, but you can at the very least be good neighbors to them and ask for neighborly respect in return. Imagine that you are buying a home. Ideally, you'd want a home in the sort of area that has good schools, low crime, and even a neighborhood watch. Luckily, gnomes are everywhere, and if you get on their good side, they will refrain from causing you any nasty trouble. They may even keep an eye on your home to safeguard it from danger, theft, or vandalism.

Casting a circle automatically blesses any place, so re-read the circle casting instructions to make sure you include each important aspect, from clearing negativity from the space to blessing it with representatives of the elements. Make sure that you sprinkle salt in water, as the representative of gnomes and the earth, in every room of the home. When you get to the heart of your ritual, you can introduce yourself by name to the gnomes that already occupy the land on which your home was built. Humbly ask them to treat your home as their own treasure, to keep it and its occupants from harm. Offer to be a good neighbor to them, and place an offering of food, drink, or bright and shiny stones outside your doorstep for them. Here is a chant you can use to raise energy and request the blessings of the gnomes.

> *Gnomes, bless this home*
> *From roof to floor*
> *From all sides and door*
> *Within and without*
> *As the wide world turns about*
> *Gnomes, bless this home.*

Thank the gnomes profusely for their help and close your magic circle. You may wish to place a penny in each corner of your home to invite the wealth of the gnomes to increase abundance of riches for you and your family. Now you've introduced yourself to your gnome neighbors and established a polite relationship so you can live harmoniously in each other's company.

Exercise to Make Friends

As with the love-drawing exercise that you found in the chapter about undines, a friendship exercise should not be aimed at a particular person. Otherwise, you may find yourself forcing somebody to do something against his or her will, which elementals don't particularly like. A well-meaning friendship exercise can lead to malicious mischief on the part of an elemental, leading your social life to blow up in a bad way. Instead, it is best to allow your qualities to draw friendship with the help of the gnomes. As with the love exercise in the chapter on undines, if you find yourself thinking of a particular person, try listing the qualities that make him or her a good friend and then thinking about what aspects of your character will need to shine to attract somebody with such qualities into your social circle.

For this exercise, you will make a friendship bracelet, so you'll need at least three colors of cotton embroidery floss. Since green is associated with the element of earth, let one of those colors be green. You can choose the other two colors to represent ideals that you think are important for friendship. Use whatever colors you think fit your purpose in your own mind, rather than what anyone else thinks each color may represent. If you're really stuck, here are some common color associations to get you started.

- *Red:* To attract a friend who is passionate and who may become more than a friend someday.

- *Orange:* To attract an energetic, happy, and positive friend.

- *Yellow:* To draw a study buddy, or a friend who is on the same wavelength as you, intellectually.

- *Green:* To attract a workout buddy, business partner, or a friend interested in growth.

- *Blue:* To draw an emotional friend who will share secrets and be deeply caring.

- *Purple:* To attract a friend interested in the spiritual world.

Cast your magic circle, face north, and ask the gnomes for their assistance in your efforts to display friendly qualities to attract better friendships into your life. There are many traditional ways to weave friendship bracelets, and you can use any of them in your work. If you have no idea how to make a friendship bracelet and missed that childhood fad, a simple braid will do just fine. As you weave, you can chant to raise energy toward your goal. Here is an example of a chant that you can use:

> *As I weave this cord from end to end,*
> *earth's gnomes will help me find a friend.*

When you are done creating your bracelet, add the caveat, "with harm to none and for the highest good of all, so mote it be." When you are done, tie the bracelet to your own wrist or ankle with a knot that you will hopefully be able to untie when you make your friendship. When you are done with your charm, you can bury it as an offering to the gnomes.

There are legends associated with giving friendship bracelets, but since they are magic, remember that you'll want to ask your friend's permission before giving him or her an enchanted object. Traditionally, a friendship bracelet is tied onto a person by a friend and then the bracelet is worn until the strings wear out and it falls off naturally. When I was a kid, they only lasted a summer. But as an adult, I find I can wear a friendship bracelet for half a year before it wears out. A friendship bracelet made by a friend is not to be removed early, unless it is an emergency, or else it may negatively affect the friendship, or so the childhood myth goes. Indeed, if I had worked many hours to make a bracelet for a childhood friend, I might be a little mad if he or she took it right off!

Close your magic circle and wear that bracelet until it falls off. Don't forget to thank the gnomes for helping you make a friend when you bury the bracelet afterward. Don't worry about removing a friendship bracelet that you made for yourself. You can certainly stay friendly with yourself without having any negative magic associated with its removal. Feel free to make additional bracelets as needed for more friends, or to attract friends with different characteristics. Don't forget to make the effort in your own life to go out and make friends, as well as to sever ties with any toxic friendships that may be blocking your social life. The gnomes are industrious elementals and they can't abide laziness. They are less likely to help you if you don't work hard toward your goals. Gnomes are slower moving, however, than sylphs for example, so be patient for them to work their magic.

Ritual to Bring Stability to Your Life

Everyone has a time in life when it seems like nothing is going well, and it feels worse when everything goes wrong at once. The devastation of a failing relationship might be bearable, but when combined with the heartbreak of losing a job and falling into ill health, one can feel spiritually lost. The situation seems hopeless. Try to look at such moments of your life as periods of flux. Changes, no matter how difficult, are temporary shifts to a new foundation. It would be nice to have stability and growth at the same time, but in reality, the disturbing transformation of growth in our lives generally happens in between the times of stability. But once those big changes occur, you can achieve a new balance and harmony. You can quickly heal and prepare for the next big life change. This ritual is one to ask the gnomes to help you find the stable element of earth inside yourself, so you can seek inner stillness and exude peace.

For this ritual, you will need to plant a tree. Ideally, you will keep one outdoors, although conceivably you could perform this ritual with an indoor plant like a bonsai tree. Select a tiny sapling, seed, or fresh cutting to prepare for planting, rather than using any old tree in the yard or a plant you already have lying around the house. As with most ritual props, it is best to procure a new item that has never been used for any other purpose before, so as to keep it clear from energies that may distract from the purpose of your ritual.

Gnomes, being of the earth, supply the life force energy that flows through plants, and their essence can be found within every tree. For this ritual, you will tell the gnomes your troubles, and ask them to lend you the same strength and stability that helps a tiny sapling grow into a sturdy tree. Cast your magic circle with the tree inside. Place the tree in the northern quadrant of your circle and knock three times on the tree, even if it is just a token knocking with one knuckle on a tiny plant, to address the gnomes of the earth energy within it.

Pour your heart out to the gnomes, tell them about all the changes and challenges going on in your life about which you wish to become more calm. In the course of everyday life, it helps to look on the bright side of things, and if you're a positive person you may have resisted the urge to complain to your friends and relatives. Take the opportunity to spill out all of your feelings, because sometimes it is cathartic to recognize that things are hard, but that they will get better. If you are the sort of person who whines a lot (like me), make this the moment that you say what you need to say so that you can stop burdening your friends and relatives with your complaints. When you are done, it is time to get the gnomes' magic moving in the direction you want.

I suggest dancing meditatively around the tree to raise energy, since the movement also symbolizes the dynamic energies that are needed for growth in between those periods of rest that you seek. Put on some gentle, relaxing music to aid your inspiration. When you feel that you've shifted your mental state into a positive one, rest your hand on the tree and thank the gnomes. If you haven't planted it already, do so as soon as you take down your circle.

The success of your tree after your ritual is a good indicator of the efficacy of your magic and whether you managed to get the blessings of the gnomes. Make sure not to neglect its care. If it grows steadily and flourishes, your prayers have been answered. If it sickens or dies, the gnomes have decided not to aid you, possibly because you need continued change in your life before it becomes healthy and spiritually sound.

Ritual to Find and Buy a Home

Looking for a new home is never fun, as often there are time and financial constraints involved, which make the process feel hurried and unsure, the opposite of the stable earth qualities one wishes to invite into a new living space. The gnomes are the ideal elementals to invoke when seeking a new home, not only because they bring the sort of prosperity that may allow you to buy one, but also because they are knowledgeable about all buildings on the earth's surface, and can help guide you to yours.

This ritual has two components. First, you will offer a prayer to the gnomes. Then you will begin searching for a place to live using a divination practice called dowsing. Dowsing is a method of finding the location of something you desire through watching the motions of a magical tool. My mother used to dowse for water in the desert using a forked stick. However, though dowsing has been traditionally used to find water, it is not relegated to being only a tool for the undines. Dowsing can be used to find any object and can involve other magical instruments like pendulums, or in the case of this ritual, copper rods. I place dowsing help confidently in the hands of the gnomes since they are very aware of all the earth's treasures.

To manufacture your dowsing rods, I suggest procuring a length of thick copper wire, about as long as your arm span. Cut the copper wire in half, and bend each piece into an L shape. To use the rods, hold one in each hand by the short branch of the L, with the long branches extending loosely forward over your hands. Extend your arms directly forward from your shoulders and allow your grip to relax, so that the rods can swing back and forth freely over the tops of your hands. When you ask the gnomes for what you seek, they can answer your prayers by causing the rods to swing together and cross each other when you arrive at the place where your treasure lies. Incidentally, these dowsing rods can also be used to find lost objects, so I find them to be a most handy tool to have around the house.

You'll begin your house-hunting journey with a prayer, after which you can use the rods to start physically hunting for your home. You can do so by using the rods over a map, driving around a neighborhood with homes for sale, or by visiting two or more homes between which you need to choose. If I'm looking at a map online, I like to pull up the map onto my laptop, and then lay the screen flat on a table so that I can hold the dowsing tool directly over it.

Below is a prayer you can use before you set out on your journey or search for a new home. You can remove lines if you wish to change the prayer to help you rent an apartment, or to buy a home that you have already found. Note that there are several lines that indicate that the will of the gnomes will be left intact if they choose not to help. Please make sure that your prayers to the gnomes always include that courtesy of freedom to keep their favor. Otherwise, you may find that you cannot trust the advice that they give.

Gnomes of earth, if you please
help me find a home with ease.
With harm to none, with your accord
give prosperity so I can afford.
For the highest good of all, as well
let the owners be inclined to sell.
With sincerest gratitude from me,
guide my hands and blessed be.

Immediately following the prayer, go searching for your new home with your dowsing rods. Trust the first moment that the rods cross to show you that you are over the right location. It can be very tempting to second-guess the movements of the rods and to override them with your hands after they have crossed. Don't overthink divination. The first answer is always the one that you receive from the source you desire, in this case the elementals, while a second or subsequent answer is just your brain playing with you. You may even want to write down the reaction of the dowsing rods you witnessed so you won't second-guess yourself later when you're making the final decision to choose the home.

There is a tradition held by Wiccans and some other magical practitioners that if you use magic to buy something, you should pay the asking price without going back and forth about the value. Such an idea may seem impossible to uphold in the modern world of real estate. However, a friend of mine has purchased property at asking price for just that reason, even though her realtor thought she had gone crazy, as she could have made an offer at a much lower cost. As soon as you have access to the home, but before you move in, be sure to perform the home blessing ritual given earlier in this chapter.

Ritual to Sell a Home

Since elementals are sentient beings, any ritual can be enhanced or even simplified by focusing on the aspect of giving an offering to them. After all, gnomes and other elementals have their own drives and are looking out for their own needs first and foremost. Interestingly, rituals for selling a home throughout history have involved burying treasures on the property, often coins or statues. Once the property has sold, the treasure is then dug up and put on an altar or place of honor to prevent the property from continuing to change hands through the industrious energy put into the rituals. One variation of a home-selling ritual following the format of underground offerings is a Catholic ritual in which the seller buries a statue of Saint Joseph. The following home-selling ritual is one that explicitly honors gnomes by making use of the cheerful garden decorations that bear their names.

For this ritual, you will need a garden gnome statue. Your statue can be small, in fact a tiny size may be preferable so that it will be easier to bury. It is okay if the statue is plastic or otherwise not decomposable, since you will be digging it up later. It is important that you buy the statue new, or make it yourself specifically for this ritual, since its energies should not be tainted with those of previous uses. That means no picking up a garden gnome from the thrift store, or repurposing one that has already been used for decoration!

Cast a magic circle with your garden gnome statue placed in the northern quadrant. With bare feet touching the earth if possible, lay your hands on the statue to charge it with the elemental earth energy of the gnomes. Below is an example of a prayer that can be chanted three times to raise the energy needed for the statue to help you with your work.

> *I invite the gnomes of the earth, if you please,*
> *for this is your fetter, with freedom to leave.*
> *And if your will be my will, so it be done.*
> *bring me buyers with money, an ample sum.*

After your chant, don't forget to add your gratitude and the caveat that none be harmed by things like loss of livelihood or free will by your ritual. For example, you can add the final line, "with harm to none, so mote it be, thank you, gnomes, and blessed be." Now, you can close your magic circle. The statue should be buried on a Wednesday, on or near a full moon, hopefully very shortly after you've charged the statue.

Bury your statue upside down in the earth so that it will work even harder to get the home sold to earn a place on your altar. You don't have to bury it very deep, but do put it somewhere that you can easily find later, like right next to the "For Sale" sign. If you are unable to find it later, you don't want to accidentally curse the property with the gnomes constantly finding more and more buyers so that ownership changes hands frequently. The home should very quickly sell to motivated buyers. Immediately after you've concluded the sale, dig up the statue, clean it off, and place it on an elemental altar or in some other place of honor so that you can remember to thank the gnomes every time you see it.

Please don't relegate your gnome to the life of a garden decoration, because if the item is stolen, it may have unintended effects for some innocent future owner of the statue. You should be very protective of any objects that you ever use in ritual work with elementals, due to their trickster nature. Always keep them from being unintentionally used by somebody who does not know that they are enchanted by elementals. If you should have need to discard any prop used in a ritual with elementals, destroy it first by casting it into a fire. Then you can bury the remains somewhere secret or scatter the ashes to wind or water.

Exercise to Increase Prosperity

The powers of the element of earth are probably most often used for material gain. In this exercise, you'll be able to ask for abundance in an ambiguous way, rather than asking specifically for a new house or car or even a sum of money. Remember, since elementals cherish their freedom, they work best for you when they are given less specific instructions. You still have to be specific about what you don't want them to do, such as harming something or feeling controlled. However, if you can give them a wide range of ways to fulfill your wishes, they are more likely to grant them quickly and with a high degree of success.

This exercise for prosperity is a common one of Italian origin, and makes use of a small lemon as a symbol of prosperity and abundance coming from the elemental realm of earth. In many myths, legends, and scriptures, the symbolism of harvesting fruit after having worked the soil is a way to show that prosperity comes through hard work, and that it comes to those for whom it is due. Citrus fruits especially are symbolic of prosperity and wealth; I have done this exercise with an orange. Ideally, you would pick the fruit yourself, but I've always used store-bought citrus since I live in a climate that is not conducive to growing them. You will also need sewing pins, the more numerous and varied in color the better. Do not use black pins for the exercise, as they can add greater challenge and adversity to your quest for riches.

This exercise for prosperity is best performed on a Sunday on or just before a full moon. Cast your magic circle, and face north to address the gnomes. Begin with a prayer to invite the gnomes to help you with monetary gain. Remember to keep things general. Here is an example prayer that you can say before you begin sticking the pins in the fruit.

> *Earth elementals I pray to you,*
> *to invite your aid for me and mine.*
>
> *As I place each pin in this charm,*
> *allow wealth to flow to me in kind.*
>
> *With harm to none, prosperity is there,*
> *I claim what I need and what I dare.*
>
> *Enough for necessities, if you please,*
> *and bring a little more to share.*

As you begin to push the pins into the fruit, be careful not to prick yourself. You can say a chant as you put each one in, like "a fortune surrounds me, good fortune within me" to raise energy for your cause. When you are done, you may thank the gnomes and close your magic circle. Place the lemon on an altar to draw prosperity. The lemon should dry out and turn into a hard, black charm that you can keep. It helps if you choose a small lemon and keep it in a cool, dry place. If your lemon instead becomes moldy, stinky, or infested with bugs, it is an indication that the gnomes have rejected your plea, and you may need to try again or resign yourself to a period of financial struggle in your life.

To dispose of a rotten charm, burn it first in a very hot outdoor fire, and then bury the ashes as an offering to the gnomes. Don't bury it without burning it. And since the pins might work their way through the soil and give somebody a rusty poke in the foot, you will need to destroy the pins first, or somehow render them harmless before burying the charm.

Ritual to Get a Job

Knot magic is also a common physical tool in ritual work. Ideally, this ritual would be performed by tying a knot in a living weeping willow tree to ask for a wish to be granted. Though you can use this technique to ask for any wish, I recommend it for a job ritual since the wish's fulfillment can be quick and straightforward, and it relates to the earth elementals' domain of material gain. To perform this ritual, get a green ribbon or length of yarn and take yourself to a willow tree to find a low-hanging and extremely supple, thin branch.

Take hold of the branch and rap on it three times with your knuckle to chase the earth elementals that live within the branch to the trunk of the tree. Tie the green ribbon just above where you knocked. There's actually nothing particularly mandatory about the ribbon for the magic to work, but I learned that it is much easier to find the branch that you enchanted when you have a marker tied to it.

Whisper your wish. In this case say, "I want to get a job" as you tie a simple knot in the branch, as if you were catching your whispered wish in the knot. Offer your thanks and then move on. When your wish is granted, you must return to the tree to untie the knot and again offer your thanks. It would be rude not to return and untie the knot after your wish has been granted, and elementals respond unpredictably and sometimes maliciously to rudeness, so please make sure that you don't neglect that final step. If your wish isn't granted promptly, return to the tree to see if the knot came out on its own. If your knot seems to have mysteriously disappeared, the gnomes may have rejected your wish. If the knot remains, you may simply have to be patient. As mentioned before, gnomes do not work as quickly as other elementals, but what they do bring to you may be more long lasting.

If you don't live in an area that has weeping willows, the ritual can be performed with any plant in which you can tie and untie a knot using the branches. Vines, drooping shrubs, or the weeping forms of other varieties of trees will do. Alternately, you can perform the entire ritual inside a magic circle, tying a knot with a green length of rope. You can enclose a flower in the knot as a token to the earth elementals, and give the flower as an offering when the knot is untied by burying it in the earth.

conclusion

*K*eith had a tough day at work and felt like he needed some fresh air and much-needed perspective. Instead of heading directly home from the office, he took a left turn and drove deep into the shady woods of the countryside. Taking a few different turns until he found an unfamiliar gravel road, he parked his car and stepped into the misty evening air. The scenic drive had soothed the immediate irritations of the day, but he still felt like something was imbalanced. Sure, he could talk about it for hours with his therapist on his dime, but taking a walk outdoors was so much more enjoyable.

The raindrops pelting his arms and hair turned into a hissing patter on the tree branches overhead as he stepped into a leafy path into the forest. Walking slowly, Keith tried to become present in the moment and to remove his mind from the complexity of his job and his human relationships. Things were so simple if he broke them down into their elemental components.

The water flowed down from the sky and moved in a river that he could sense from a faraway roar. The wet earth beneath his feet cradled decaying leaves and nurtured new tree saplings that shot optimistically up toward the sky. The air was crisp and alive, smelling like dirt and cedar. A fire of life and creation dwelled within Keith's heart and within every creeping thing in the forest, from ants climbing up the trees to worms writhing in the damp forest path.

Feeling calm, Keith stopped and rested on a fallen tree that was sheltered from the rain. He focused on his breath and his heart rate, feeling his body rhythms slowing from the frantic pace of the city life. Keith began to meditate about how every element in nature commingled to create a perfect balance. One element could not exist without the other. Keith wondered if there was an imbalance of elements in his own life. Perhaps in his constant drive for purity and perfection, he had tried to do something impossible. There is no way for the earth to exist in a forest without the rain, wind, and life that makes it what it is.

Keith felt like his life was too focused on his job and earthly matters. There was too much focus on gaining money and a firm footing of financial security, without enjoying the blessed rain of his relationships with friends and family, the sacred inspiration of creativity, or the burning fire of spiritual discovery. He didn't feel the way he did when he was a small boy anymore, when the world seemed full of promise and it was impossible to slow down and dwell on just one thing.

Keith realized that he was so relaxed that his eyes were closed. He opened them and saw that the rain had stopped, but droplets *of water were still falling in the glow of twilight. A creature flashed by his head, startling Keith. Was it a bat hunting for insects? It seemed like it could be anything in this magical forest, perhaps even a creature from deep in the past, or one that had not yet been discovered.*

Keith regarded his surroundings with new eyes. The tree next to him had knots that looked like a smiling face. He picked up a smooth rock that looked like it was in the shape of a round woman without a face, frozen in stone for all time. He spied an acorn and took it into his hand as well. It looked like a hat for a small faerie, or perhaps a boat for an even tinier being. He smiled and put the treasures in his pocket. He had found his perspective. Keith decided that he needed to create a garden outside his home so that he could find a little solace in nature without driving out into the boonies. Perhaps then he could offer some plants and flowers to return the favor to the faerie and elemental life in the forest that had lifted his spirits.

If you haven't already experienced the reality of faeries and elementals helping you in your everyday life, I hope that you will start experimenting with some of the practices I've set forth in this book to help you work with them. Start at the beginning and work your way through, or pick what you think is the most simple meditation and wait to see how it improves your life. Don't be afraid to be observant. Seeing real success in your actual life through elemental exercises and faerie encounters will help you gain new hope and belief in the magical world. It isn't enough to simply learn the lore, although stories about elementals and faeries are always fascinating.

I've shown you contemporary ways to use elementals for purposes and to appease faeries so that you can gain their help and sometimes even friendship. Now it is up to you to test for yourself and look at the results. Imagine making friends with creatures that can help you find or keep true love, gain money and happiness in your work life, and feel better about your spiritual life. Elementals can help you gain power and knowledge about your own inner spiritual development. Faeries can teach you to be reverent and curious about the natural world. Elementals and faeries can be like your best friends and your parents at the same time. They know your deepest fears, and they will support you in your highest hopes and dreams. You are only limited by your imagination.

Not everything in the universe is yet explained, and we should take joy in the everyday mysteries of discovery. Can you remember being a small child and reveling in the delight of fantastical stories? You wanted to know how everything worked and just what needed to be done to achieve each of your goals. Learning was a process of not only gathering facts, but finding your place in the world. You still have a place in the world that is evolving every day. Bold and fascinating stories are being told anew in the minds of those who work with faeries and elementals, and in the natural world around them. Will you dare to be one of them?

So cast off the shackles of disbelief, adulthood, and all things ordinary and well-known. You are an explorer of new realms, perhaps a discoverer of new creatures nobody has ever seen before. The elementals can be seen inside you and in the faces and hearts of everyone you meet. Faeries don't have to just be in storybooks anymore—they can be on the tip of your tongue and right before your eyes. Let others see the glow of how the magical world of elementals and faeries has affected you, and you will be a welcome ambassador for elementals and faeries in the mundane world.

glossary

Amulet: An object from the natural world that is carried or worn as a protective charm. Amulets can be gifts from elementals or faeries, and can protect against them if needed.

Astral plane: A plane of existence on which ideas and goals must be created before they can manifest in the physical world. The astral plane is affected by ritual, energy, the mind of a magical practitioner, and elementals and faeries.

Athame: A black-handled ritual knife that is associated with air elementals. It is used to direct energy and threaten negative spirits in a ritual context. An athame is never used to actually cut anything in the physical world.

Besom: A ritual broom used before casting a circle to sweep away all negative or unintended energies.

Ceremonial magic: A twentieth-century Western magical system originating in Europe and based upon Kabbalah.

Chalice: Also called cup, a chalice is a ritual tool used to contain holy water or a beverage used for partaking or offering during a ritual. A chalice is associated with water elementals.

Charge: To imbue an object, person, or idea with magical energy toward manifesting a goal.

Circle: A ritual space constructed temporarily to contain energy and protect what exists within.

Correspondences: Connections between ideas and symbols that are made and often shared between magical practitioners, to add to the power of concepts in the mind of a person casting a spell or performing a ritual.

Divination: Using ritual tools to obtain psychic information or advice about the past, present, or future.

Elementalism: The practice of worshiping elementals as deities.

Elementals: Energetic archetypes of earth, air, fire, and water. Elementals are personification of the four powerful puzzle pieces of the universe, and they are often believed to be sentient beings.

Faeries: Energetic or spiritual beings that are a personification of natural phenomenon.

Magic: Change that is initiated within a person or in the real world around a person that aligns with the person's will.

Pentacle: A five-pointed star surrounded by a circle, representing the elementals and spirit. Also, a ritual tool bearing the same symbol.

Pentagram: A five-pointed star representing the elementals and spirit.

Prayer: A message, usually expressed in words, addressed toward at least one higher power. Prayers are used to confer praise or gratitude, or to request intercession regarding a specific need or desire.

Psychic: A person who obtains information from a supernatural source, or senses by means other than the five natural senses.

Ritual: A ceremony that takes a prescribed form to accomplish the desired spiritual goals or magical effects in a predictable way every time.

Scrying: A method of divination in which the practitioner gazes into a tool or substance to see visions in the tool or in the mind's eye.

Sigil: A symbol, usually made from lettering, that represents a greater concept. Sigils are created to focus the mind on a complex idea during a ritual or spell.

Spell: A discrete act of magic performed for a specific goal. A spell is often performed in the context of a ritual, and may produce or make use of magical props to focus the mind and energy.

Spirit: An overarching term for a spiritual entity that includes faeries, elves, and ghosts, among others.

Talisman: A magical object that is created by a person to have a specific effect on a person who chooses to wear it. For example, talismans are often created to confer protection or luck upon the bearer.

Thoughtform: An idea created by a magical practitioner on the astral plane that is fueled by spiritual energy to carry out a specific task (such as a spell's goal) before it dissipates.

Wand: Usually a wooden stick, a wand is used to direct energy during a spell or ritual. A wand is usually associated with fire elementals.

bibliography

Arrowsmith, Nancy. *Field Guide to the Little People: A Curious Journey Into the Hidden Realm of Elves, Faeris, Hobgoblins & Other Not-So-Mythical Creatures.* Woodbury, MN: Llewellyn Publications, 2009.

Leland, Charles Godfrey. *Aradia: The Gospel of the Witches.* Calgary, Alberta, Canada: Theophania Publishing, 2010.

Mackenzie, Vicki. *Why Buddhism? Westerners in Search of Wisdom.* Hammersmith, London: Thorsons, 2003.

McCoy, Edain. *A Witch's Guide to Faery Folk.* Woodbury, MN: Llewellyn Publications, 2010.

Melville, Francis. *The Book of Faeries: A Guide to the World of Elves, Pixies, Goblins, and Other Magic Spirits.* Hauppauge, NY: Quarto Inc., 2002.

Moon, Janell. *How to Pray Without Being Religious: Finding Your Own Spiritual Path.* Hammersmith, London: Thorsons, 2004.

Moura, Ann. *Green Magic: The Sacred Connection to Nature.* Woodbury, MN: Llewellyn Publications, 2010.

Om, Mya. *The Un-Spell Book: Energy Essentials for Mastering Magick.* Woodbury, MN: Llewellyn Publications, 2010.

Osho. *The ABC of Enlightenment: A Spiritual Dictionary for the Here and Now.* Hammersmith, London: Element, 2003.

Virtue, Doreen. *Faeries 101: An Introduction to Connecting, Working and Healing with the Faeries and Other Elementals.* Carlsbad, CA: Hay House, 2011.

To Write to the Author

If you wish to contact the author or would like more information about this book, please write to the author in care of Llewellyn Worldwide, and we will forward your request. Both the author and publisher appreciate hearing from you and learning of your enjoyment of this book and how it has helped you. Llewellyn Worldwide cannot guarantee that every letter written to the author can be answered, but all will be forwarded. Please write to:

Alexandra Chauran
℅ Llewellyn Worldwide
2143 Wooddale Drive
Woodbury, MN 55125-2989

Please enclose a self-addressed stamped envelope for reply, or $1.00 to cover costs. If outside the USA, enclose an international postal reply coupon.